Leopard Gecko

2nd Edition

Frank Indiviglio

BICENTENNIAL
1807
WILEY
2007
BICENTENNIAL

Wiley Publishing, Inc.

Library of Congress Cataloging-in-Publication Data:
Indiviglio, Frank.
    Leopard gecko / Frank Indiviglio. — 2nd ed.
        p. cm. — (Your happy healthy pet)
    Includes bibliographical references and index.
    ISBN 978-0-470-03792-8 (cloth : alk. paper)
    1. Leopard geckos as pets. I. Title.
    SF459.G35I53 2007
    639.3'952—dc22
                                                    2007002524

Printed in the United States of America

10   9   8   7   6   5   4   3   2   1

2nd Edition

Book design by Melissa Auciello-Brogan
Cover design by Michael J. Freeland
Book production by Wiley Publishing, Inc. Composition Services
Wiley Bicentennial Logo: Richard J. Pacifico

About the Author

Frank Indiviglio is a biologist and environmental lawyer who has spent most of his life working with animals at the Bronx and Staten Island Zoos in New York City. His field research projects in Latin America have involved animals ranging from anacondas to leatherback turtles, and he has been a biology and natural history teacher at Science Development, Inc., and Columbia Preparatory School in Manhattan.

Frank tends to focus on the "less appreciated" animal species but is interested in them all. He has written four books and numerous magazine articles on the captive care and natural history of invertebrates, fishes, amphibians, reptiles, birds, and mammals.

About Howell Book House

Since 1961, Howell Book House has been America's premier publisher of pet books. We're dedicated to companion animals and the people who love them, and our books reflect that commitment. Our stable of authors—training experts, veterinarians, breeders, and other authorities—is second to none. And we've won more Maxwell Awards from the Dog Writers Association of America than any other publisher.

As we head toward the half-century mark, we're more committed than ever to providing new and innovative books, along with the classics our readers have grown to love. This year, we're launching several exciting new initiatives, including redesigning the Howell Book House logo and revamping our biggest pet series, Your Happy Healthy Pet™, with bold new covers and updated content. From bringing home a new puppy to competing in advanced equestrian events, Howell has the titles that keep animal lovers coming back again and again.

Contents

Part I: The Leopard Gecko's World   9

Chapter 1: What Is a Gecko?   11
Lizards as Pets   12
How Geckos Are Like Other Reptiles   14
How Geckos Are Different   14
Humans and Geckos   18

Chapter 2: What Makes the Leopard Gecko Special?   20
All in the Subfamily   21
Natural Habitat of the Leopard Gecko   23
Is a Leopard Gecko the Right Pet for You?   24
The Perfect Lizard Pet   26

Chapter 3: Colors, Patterns, and Phases   28
The Language of Variation   28

Part II: Caring for Your Leopard Gecko   37

Chapter 4: Choosing Your Leopard Gecko   38
Where to Shop   38
The Ideal Age   41
Re-grown Tails   42
When You've Chosen Your Leopard Gecko   44
Environmental Ethics   46
Captive Bred vs. Wild Caught   46

Chapter 5: Housing Your Leopard Gecko   50
The Vivarium   50
Understanding and Avoiding Salmonella   58
Building a Custom Habitat   60
Cleaning Your Leopard Gecko's Habitat   61

Chapter 6: Feeding Your Leopard Gecko   63
What to Feed   63
How to Feed   64
Vitamins and Minerals   67
How to Keep and Gut Load Crickets   70
Wild-Caught Invertebrates   71
Water   72

Chapter 7: Keeping Your Leopard Gecko Healthy   74
Choosing a Veterinarian   74
Common Health Problems   75

Part III: Behavior and Breeding   83

Chapter 8: Your Leopard Gecko's Behavior   84
Hunting   84
Shedding   85
Territoriality   86
Home Alone   87
Mating   88
Nesting   89
Hiding   89
Your Gecko's Personality   90
The Outside World   91
Change of Seasons   93
Handling a Leopard Gecko   94

Chapter 9: Breeding Leopard Geckos   96
Sexing Leopard Geckos   96
Breeding Age   99
The Right Time of Year   101
The Mating   104

Chapter 10: Hatching and Raising Baby Geckos   107
Choosing an Incubation Medium   107
Choosing Egg Containers   109
Moving the Eggs   110
Caring for the Eggs   111
Maintaining Moisture Levels during Incubation   113
Maintaining Proper Temperatures   114
The Hatching   117
Raising Young Leopard Geckos   120

Appendix: Learning More About Your Leopard Gecko   121
Some Good Books   121
Magazines   121
Herpetological Societies   122
Internet Resources   123

Index   125

Shopping List

You'll need to do a bit of stocking up before you bring your Leopard gecko home. Below is a basic list of must-have supplies. For more detailed information on the selection of each item below, consult chapter 5. For specific guidance on what food you'll need, review chapter 6.

- ☐ Tank
- ☐ Tank cover
- ☐ Tank lid clamps
- ☐ Tank stand
- ☐ Heat lamp or reflector with incandescent bulb
- ☐ Heat tape or heat mat
- ☐ Thermostat
- ☐ Thermometer
- ☐ Sand, paper towels, or other substrate
- ☐ UV fluorescent light (if you keep live plants)

- ☐ Night-viewing light bulb
- ☐ Rocks, driftwood, and other naturalistic cage decorations
- ☐ Live or plastic plants
- ☐ Hide box
- ☐ Water dish
- ☐ Food dish
- ☐ Live crickets, superworms, mealworms, and waxworms
- ☐ Vitamin and mineral supplements
- ☐ Plastic spoon for removing feces and dead insects

There are likely to be a few other items that, depending upon your vivarium setup, you may wish to pick up before bringing your gecko home. Use the blank spaces at the end of this list to note any additional items you'll be shopping for.

- ☐ _____
- ☐ _____
- ☐ _____
- ☐ _____
- ☐ _____
- ☐ _____
- ☐ _____

Pet Sitter's Guide

We can be reached at (___) ___ - _____ Cellphone (___)_____-_____

_____

We will return on _____ (date) at _____ (approximate time)

Other individual to contact in case of emergency _____

_____

Lizard species _____

Care Instructions

In the following blank lines, let the sitter know what to feed, how much, and when; what tasks need to be performed daily; and what weekly tasks they'll be responsible for.

Morning_____

_____

_____

_____

_____

Evening _____

_____

_____

_____

_____

Other tasks and special instructions _____

_____

_____

_____

_____

Part I
The Leopard Gecko's World

The Leopard Gecko

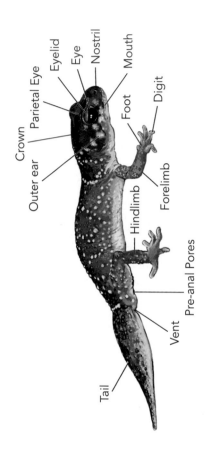

Crown
Parietal Eye
Eyelid
Eye
Nostril
Mouth
Outer ear
Foot
Digit
Hindlimb
Forelimb
Pre-anal Pores
Vent
Tail

Chapter 1

What Is a Gecko?

Geckos are lizards. When it comes to diversity, lizards are the most successful of the reptiles—nearly 4,000 species have been described.

The family of lizards to which the Leopard gecko belongs is known as the Gekkonidae. This incredibly diverse and successful group of lizards contains more than 800 species, with new ones being described by scientists each year. It's a complicated family with many interesting twists and turns. The level of diversity in this one branch of lizards is so complex and specialized that it can inspire and dazzle. This complexity makes geckos very exciting to study and to keep as pets.

Geckos live in many types of habitats around the world, ranging from searing, dry deserts to lush, cool mountain forests. There are many different types of geckos. The most exciting thing about geckos is their diversity. Some are unique, odd creatures. Some are virtual living jewels.

Geckos have been successful in colonizing the globe because they are able to exploit many types of habitats. Many gecko species have adapted to highly specialized niches in their surroundings, which are called microhabitats. For example, a South African *Rhotropus* species can live exclusively in rock cracks, while another species lives exclusively on the ground. Both species inhabit the same location, each exploiting specific microhabitats.

Some types of geckos are found only in the wild, while others turn up in pet shops or are offered by breeders.

Is a Lizard Right for You?

- How much space are you willing to devote to your lizard's cage?
- Can you afford the costs associated with lizard ownership, including food, equipment, electricity, and veterinary care?
- If you will have more than one lizard, do you have room to house them separately, if necessary?
- Will you be willing to feed your lizard insects?
- Will you be able to provide your pet with a varied and nutritious diet?
- Is a reptile veterinarian available nearby?
- Will your children and other family members be willing to learn how to properly care for a delicate lizard?
- Who will care for your lizard while you are away on business or vacation?
- Can you commit to caring for a pet who may live for more than 20 years?
- Does the risk of Salmonella present a special threat to anyone in your household (see page 58 for more on Salmonella)?
- Will dogs, cats, or other pets be a threat to your lizard?

Lizards as Pets

No one knows exactly when human beings began keeping lizards as pets, but we can surmise that the practice started a long time ago. It is clear from both art and scientific literature that humans have been fascinated by lizards for thousands of years. Lizards feature prominently in the artistic and religious traditions of the ancient inhabitants of many areas, including Australia, North America, and Southeast Asia.

In the late twentieth century, people in both the United States and Canada began to develop a strong fascination with keeping lizards as pets. While in the

1960s and 1970s geckos were only rarely seen in pet stores, a small lizard called the Anole was common. These little lizards were sold as pets for children. There was also a trend in the 1950s for women to "wear" Anoles on their clothing. The lizard would be attached to a pin with a small leash. Unfortunately, little was known of their requirements in captivity, and most quickly died.

In the last decade, there has been a huge increase in the popularity of lizards as pets (not as pins) with both children and adults. Consequently, a number of lizard species are now available to the average reptile fan. What these animals need to thrive in captivity is well known, resulting in an ever-increasing number of captive breeding successes. In some cases, this interest in lizards has led to the

Many people like lizards because they look like little dinosaurs.

over-collection of wild specimens, but in others, large-scale captive breeding has led to a decrease in collectiing.

Many people like lizard pets because they look like tiny dinosaurs. And all lizards—in fact, all life—can trace their ancestry back to those early reptiles. The natural history of the lizard is fascinating, and it takes us back to nearly the very beginning of life itself.

The gecko of today is the evolutionary descendent of those reptiles who survived beyond the dinosaurs. Geckos have a lot in common with their prehistoric ancestors, and little has changed in their biology over the eons. In fact, geckos are among the most primitive lizards alive today. We can appreciate our pet geckos as not only links to nature, but as links to our own very distant past.

Lizards have very specific care requirements, but, unlike dogs or cats, they can be left for a couple of days without the need for someone to come in and take care of them. Lights can be put on timers, and food items and water can be left in feeding dishes to supply all their needs while you are away. They do not need attention or affection to thrive. They are quiet. They do not smell. They also do not affect people with allergies.

How Geckos Are Like Other Reptiles

There are many traits geckos have in common with their reptilian cousins. With the exception of certain species of Sea turtles (which, through a unique mechanism, are able to internally generate heat), all reptiles, including geckos, are ectothermic. This means they are unable to internally regulate their own body temperature the way that mammals and birds can. Instead, geckos rely on outside sources to stay warm or cool, and must move from place to place to keep their body temperature just right. In the early morning, a gecko will seek a warm, sunlit place to heat up his body. When the sun becomes too hot, the gecko will move to a shady area so he can cool down.

Taste and Smell

Like other lizards, geckos use their tongue to "taste" things in their environment. The long, broad tongue reaches out to pick up molecules from their environment. These molecules are brought back into the mouth, where they come into contact with the vomeronasal, or Jacobson's organ, located above the palate. This organ enables the gecko to determine the exact nature of whatever he has tasted—whether it is an unrecognized insect, an obstacle in his path, or your hand.

Skin

Geckos and other lizards have an outer layer of skin, known as the epidermis, made up of keratin. This layer is shed in patches as the gecko grows. Many lizards consume the shed skin, while others do not.

They also have an inner layer of skin, known as the dermis, that contains a large number of blood vessels and pigment-producing cells. Both layers of gecko skin are very delicate and tear easily. However, some lizards, such as the Armadillo lizard (*Cordylus cataphractus*), have hard, armorlike skin that offers excellent protection from predators.

How Geckos Are Different

Despite their reptilian characteristics, you've probably noticed that geckos look somewhat different from other lizards. This is because they have several distinctive traits.

Geckos have a triangular head and a distinctive neck. Many, but not all, also have adhesive foot pads. This is a Day gecko.

Head

One of the easiest traits to spot is the construction of the gecko's head. Geckos tend to have a triangular-shaped head with a discernible neck that attaches their unusual head to their body, while most other lizards have a more streamlined, V-shaped head that seems to flow right into their body.

Feet

The feet of many geckos have adhesive pads on the bottom that enable the gecko to stick to just about any surface. These pads, called lamellae, are covered with thousands of minute hairlike setae, which are further subdivided into microscopic structures known as spatulae. These unique structures enable geckos to cling to even the smallest irregularities on a climbing surface.

In some species, such as the Tokay gecko (*Gekko gecko*), the lamellae also seem to create suction through the buildup of static electricity. Not all geckos have these pads, but the ones that do can hold on pretty tightly when they want to—even when they are upside down.

Tail

One of the gecko's most distinctive characteristics is his tail. Rather than being long and narrow, as on other lizards, a gecko's tail is usually narrow at the base, thick in the middle, and narrow at the tip. Like some other lizards, many species of geckos use their tail to store fat for those times when food is scarce.

Just like certain other lizards, a gecko's tail is autonomous. That means he can detach his tail, usually along preexisting fracture planes in the bones, to distract predators. Special muscles make the detached tail wiggle and writhe, keeping the predator from noticing that the best part of the meal is getting away! Nearby blood vessels are quickly shut down so that blood loss is minimal.

The gecko's autonomous tail is one reason that it's so important to handle geckos carefully—their tails are easily detached when the geckos are roughly handled, even by well-meaning humans.

Voice

Many gecko species are able to vocalize. Of those that can, the male gecko uses his voice to warn away intruders to his territory and also to attract a mate; the female can also produce sounds. Both sexes may also produce loud alarm calls when captured, hoping to startle an enemy into momentarily letting go. This ability makes geckos a somewhat unique family in the lizard world, because most other lizards are relatively silent.

Male Tokay geckos have a loud, distinctive call from which their name is derived.

The Singing Gecko

Perhaps the most well known of the gecko vocalists is the Tokay gecko (*Gekko gecko*). They can reach 12 inches in length and have a bite to match their impressive size. In addition to being more than willing to bite, they do not release their grip easily. Tokay geckos are also very fast and can climb walls easily.

These geckos quite often move into people's homes in their native Southeast Asia and in their introduced ranges throughout the world, such as southern Florida. The loud, territorial call of the male sounds like "*Tokay! Tokay!*," and has given the species its common name.

Male Tokay geckos are strictly nocturnal, and may repeat this call incessantly, often at approximately 4 a.m.—thereby becoming rather unwelcome alarm clocks.

Some years ago in New York City, pet stores began renting Tokay geckos to people seeking to rid their apartments of cockroaches, which happen to be among the Tokay gecko's favorite foods. However, the lizards' vocal talents soon put an end to this unique trend in urban pest control.

Tokay geckos are still quite common in the pet trade, but you are better off leaving these stocky, aggressive fellows to very experienced hobbyists.

Eyes

The eyes of the gecko vary depending on the species. Most geckos are nocturnal (active mostly at night) and have pupils that look like vertical slits when viewed in the daylight. These nocturnal geckos have very strong night vision, and those narrow pupils will dilate to encompass nearly the entire eye. A few geckos are diurnal, meaning they are most active during the day. These geckos have round pupils that look somewhat like ours.

The majority of gecko species have eyelids that are fused, and therefore cannot blink, which makes them similar to snakes but different from most other reptiles. However, some species of geckos—such as the Leopard gecko—do have moveable eyelids.

All geckos actually lick their eye area with their tongue. While scientists aren't completely sure why they do this, many suspect this is the gecko's way of keeping the eyes clean.

Ears

Gecko ears are another fascinating part of the lizard's anatomy. If you hold certain gecko species up to the light, you can actually see through their ear canals out to the other side! But don't let that fool you into thinking there is not much in there. The gecko ear is complicated, and geckos can hear as well as or better than most other lizards.

Geckos need good hearing to be able to effectively communicate with members of their own species. It's also possible that they use their hearing to avoid predators and when hunting for prey.

Endolymphatic Sacs

Some species of geckos in the subfamily Gekkoninae, such as the various Day geckos, have large sacs on both sides of their neck. These sacs are reservoirs for calcium. Scientists aren't sure why some geckos have these bulging sacs, but, because they are largest in females and increase in size during the breeding season, it is surmised that they could be used to help female geckos form egg shells. The smaller sacs of the males and nonbreeding females may help in the metabolism of calcium.

Diet

One characteristic that all geckos share is a penchant for eating bugs. Without exception, all gecko species consume insects and other invertebrates, such as spiders and sow bugs.

Some will eat other foods as well. Day geckos, for example, have been known to drink nectar and lap at rotting fruit as an occasional treat. Larger species, such as the Tokay gecko, will also eat small mammals, nestling birds, frogs, snakes, and other lizards.

Humans and Geckos

Geckos have lived in close association with humans for a long time. Geckos in various parts of the world can be found cohabitating with humans in their dwellings. These are not "pet" geckos per se, but rather wild lizards who have wandered into humans' homes in pursuit of insects. Because geckos are so good at eating bugs, they are welcome in most homes. In fact, in Malaysia, having a Tokay gecko in your home is considered good luck.

Several smaller gecko species, known collectively as "house geckos," are notorious stowaways on ships and in luggage, and have established themselves far outside their natural habitats. A number of species from Europe, Asia, and the Caribbean, including the Indo-Pacific gecko, the Mediterranean gecko, and the Ashy gecko, have thriving populations in Florida and other southern portions of the United States.

In the southwestern United States, geckos lived closely with Native Americans in a desert environment. These geckos, most likely Banded geckos, were often the subject of Native American art. Their images have survived in the form of rock art, pottery, jewelry, and fetish objects. The stylized representation of a gecko shown on so much Native American art has even come to represent the spirit of the North American southwest.

Because many species are easy to breed in captivity and even easier to keep, geckos, in particular, have grown in popularity. Nearly every pet store in the United States that sells lizards now carries geckos. The Leopard gecko is the most popular gecko pet and is readily available to any lizard keeper.

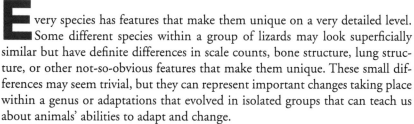

Chapter 2

What Makes the Leopard Gecko Special?

Every species has features that make them unique on a very detailed level. Some different species within a group of lizards may look superficially similar but have definite differences in scale counts, bone structure, lung structure, or other not-so-obvious features that make them unique. These small differences may seem trivial, but they can represent important changes taking place within a genus or adaptations that evolved in isolated groups that can teach us about animals' abilities to adapt and change.

The chart on page 21 shows how taxonomists classify Leopard geckos. The class Reptilia tells us that Leopard geckos are reptiles. The order Squamata tells us they are in the group of snakes, lizards, and worm lizards. The suborder Sauria tells us they are specifically lizards, not snakes or worm lizards. The infra-order Gekkota tells us they are in a group of lizards that includes geckos, night lizards, and pygopods. The family Gekkonidae is the family of all geckos. The subfamily Eublepharinae is the whole group of primitive, specialized geckos with eyelids.

The genus is where things get very specific. The genus *Eublepharis* narrows the gecko's characteristics down to very similar details that make a group of geckos closely related. And the species *macularius* means we are talking only about Leopard geckos.

Classifying the Leopard Gecko

Class:	Reptilia
Order:	Squamata
Suborder:	Sauria
Infraorder:	Gekkota
Family:	Gekkonidae
Subfamily:	Eublepharinae
Genus:	*Eublepharis*
Species:	*macularius*

All in the Subfamily

The Leopard gecko shares the subfamily Eubleparinae with Banded geckos and Fat-tailed geckos. These lizards are the most primitive geckos. Members of this family are the only geckos to have functional eyelids, which is why they are called eyelid geckos. They all have the genus name *Eublepharis,* which means "true eyelids." The Leopard gecko's species name, *macularius,* means "spotted."

In all other Gekkonidae species, the eyes are covered by a transparent cap, called the spectacle. The spectacle is fused to the eyelids, rendering the eyes permanently "open." Unable to blink, most geckos use their long, flexible tongues to clean the spectacle—which can be quite surprising to a new pet owner!

Leopard gecko eyes also have elongated, slit-shaped pupils. Diurnal geckos (those who are active during daylight) have round pupils. If you look closely at a Leopard gecko's eyes, you will notice the vertical slit. The pupil opens widely in the dark to let the maximum amount of light into the eye, but closes to a very tiny slit in bright light.

Another feature unique to this family of geckos is that they all lack the adhesive lamellae on their toes that enable other geckos to climb walls and glass. A common misconception about geckos is that they all have sticky feet and can climb on any type of surface. Some geckos do have adhesive lamellae, but eyelid geckos never developed them. Because their

---

Did You Know?

In this genus, only the Leopard gecko, *Eublepharis macularius,* appears in the pet trade. *Eublepharis angramainyu* is one of the largest members and is native to Iran, Iraq, Syria, and Turkey. *Eublepharis fuscus* may be the largest of all. This gecko lives in India, and there are published reports of her reaching 10 inches from snout to vent. A 10-inch gecko is a true giant of the genus.

Leopard geckos have eyelids, but they still use their tongue to keep their eyes clean.

natural habitat is dry and rocky, lamellae on their feet might make traveling difficult or hamper digging.

In addition, the eyelid geckos lay soft-shelled eggs, rather than the more typical hard-shelled ones of other geckos.

The Leopard gecko does, however, share many characteristics common to other family members. Like most eyelid geckos, her body is cylindrical with a large, distinct head topped by protruding eyes. Although her skin has granulations, it feels quite soft to the touch and is fairly thin. The skin is heavily patterned. Patterning in nature breaks up shapes, which helps protect and conceal the gecko from predators. In the home vivarium, the colors and patterns make for an unusually attractive pet. Even the blandest of Leopard geckos is a stunning animal. The texture of the Leopard gecko's skin is bumpy, perhaps another way to help avoid detection.

The Leopard gecko has developed a large tail, in which she is able to store a lot of fat. In her harsh native climate, food can be quite plentiful for short periods and then disappear for weeks. A fat-storage system can, therefore, be lifesaving. A healthy Leopard gecko will always have a chunky tail.

With these adaptations, Leopard geckos are very suitable animals for captive care. They are hardy, prolific, gentle, and attractive. It is no wonder hobbyists often call them the perfect reptile pet.

Natural Habitat of the Leopard Gecko

The Leopard gecko's native habitat stretches from Iraq in the west through Iran, Afghanistan, and Pakistan, terminating in northwestern India. The landscape inhabited by the Leopard gecko is dry and rocky. The terrain ranges from sandy gravel to hard clay soil with a sandy covering. Vegetation consists of bushes and grasses.

They are terrestrial lizards, living on and under the ground. They rarely climb, and when they do, they can be somewhat clumsy. Leopard geckos prefer to be under rocks and in holes underground. They remain hidden during the day and become active at dusk.

The heavily patterned, bumpy skin helps the gecko conceal herself in the wild.

Is a Leopard Gecko the Right Pet for You?

New pet owners, even responsible adults, commonly underestimate the commitment of time and money that even a single animal will require. Although Leopard geckos are among the least "labor intensive" of the reptiles, owning one is a long-term obligation that requires serious thought. Let's take a look at what's involved.

Time

Leopard geckos may live up to 25 years in captivity, so their long-term care must be considered. Zoos will not accept unwanted animals and private placement is not likely, given this species' wide availability and low cost.

Daily care involves carefully assessing your pet's condition and behavior, spot-cleaning feces, removing dead food insects, changing the water bowl or spraying the tank, and checking the functioning of the lighting and heating equipment.

Periodic chores include cleaning the vivarium glass, changing the substrate, replacing bulbs and heating equipment, and caring for any live plants.

If you keep more than one lizard, you must plan for the possibility of aggression, which will necessitate additional tanks. Observation of your lizard becomes more important, and time consuming, when several are housed together. Captive reproduction, worthwhile as it might be, requires an additional commitment of time and space.

Expense

The costs of cages, aquariums, light fixtures, heating units, and related items can be high or reasonable, depending upon your tastes and the size of your collection, but they will certainly involve an initial outlay of money.

Their native regions get cold during the winter months, and these geckos take refuge underground from early winter to early spring. In the Peshawar area of Pakistan, the temperature can drop to 41°F (5°C) at night and rise to 59°F (15°C) during the day in January. In the summer, by contrast, things can get quite hot. During the hottest months, temperatures can reach 104°F (40°C) during the day and drop to 77°F (25°C) at night.

Veterinary care must be planned for, because veterinarians with reptile expertise are far from common. Routine care and medications for lizards are comparable in price to those for birds and mammals, and surgeries can be phenomenally expensive. Routine office visits in large cities will average $100.

Food insects are quite expensive to purchase, and breeding is a time consuming (and, in the case of crickets, noisy!) prospect. Feeding involves more than just supplying crickets, as well. A variety of food insects must be located and purchased or bred. Most food insects should themselves be housed and fed a nutritious diet before being offered to pets.

Other Considerations

All reptiles are potential carriers of Salmonella and other microorganisms (see "Understanding and Avoiding Salmonella" on page 58). You must consider the associated health risks, especially if you live with young, elderly, or immune-compromised people. Pet ownership under such circumstances places a grave responsibility upon your shoulders.

You must also consider how to accommodate your pet when you are away from home for extended periods. Care for reptiles is often harder to arrange than for more common pets. Ideally, a trusted friend or family member would help out, but you may need to arrange for a paid service or for boarding.

Since your pet may live for 25 years or longer, you should think about your own long-term plans, and decide, if possible, whether a gecko will fit in with your changing priorities. If you have a sizable collection, it is especially important to consider the effect of life changes such as moving or marriage.

Emergencies will happen, too—generally at the worst possible time. Plan for animal and equipment problems, and give thought to your own ability to handle them while juggling the rest of your life's responsibilities.

In the wild, Leopard geckos have many enemies. Nocturnal hunters such as foxes, snakes, and birds of prey all can and do exploit Leopard geckos. Long periods of drought, heavy rains, and people encroaching into the Leopard gecko's habitat all play a role in restricting this gecko's ability to survive in the wild. The life span of a Leopard gecko in the wild is unknown, but is certainly shorter than life in captivity.

Reptile Senses

Lizards, including geckos, have a well-developed sense of taste. Along with the ability to taste with their tongues, most lizards have what is known as a vomeronasal, or Jacobson's organ, in their mouth. This organ is located in the roof of the mouth and is distinct from both the sense of taste (which, as in people, is a function of taste buds on the tongue) and what we traditionally think of as the sense of smell.

In lizards, the sense of smell operates as in most animals: airborne molecules are sensed and analyzed as they enter the nostrils along with the air taken in for respiration. The vomeronasal organ, which snakes and some mammals also have, enables them to sense nonairborne chemical molecules in the environment.

The organ actually functions as a "sixth sense," enabling the animal to detect predators, prey, and potential mates, even when such are not within sight. Snakes and some of the more recently evolved lizards, such as the Monitor lizard, rely very heavily on the information received through the vomeronasal organ.

The Perfect Lizard Pet

Leopard geckos are as close to a perfect lizard pet as you can get. Besides the fact that they are attractive and easy to care for, they are the most widely captive-produced geckos in the world. Breeders produce thousands every year to supply the pet trade. This captive production is important for several reasons. The first is that they are not taken from the wild. Wild-caught geckos present a whole range of problems, from environmental concerns to issues about the animals' health and behavior.

Smaller lizards such as Leopard geckos have several other advantages that make them ideal to keep in the home. While many lizards can be tricky to keep, and some grow very large, this is not the case with the Leopard gecko.

Leopard geckos also come in a wide array of stunning colors and patterns, as will be explained in chapter 3.

Availability

Another reason Leopard geckos are nearly perfect pets is their availability to the average person. Many pet stores in the United States sell them. Reptile expos, held year-round in many cities, always have several Leopard gecko breeders in attendance. Reptile magazines advertise many breeders, often with photos depicting stunning animals. Even surfing the Internet will yield many choices for buying or trading Leopard geckos.

Easy Handling

Physically, Leopard geckos are the perfect size for a pet lizard. They grow to an approximate length of 8 to 10 inches. This size allows for comfortable handling. The body is fairly heavy and thick, giving the animal a sturdy feel. Small children can hold a Leopard gecko without the gecko intimidating them.

The Leopard gecko's space requirements are minimal. The habitat need not be enormous for these geckos to thrive. A common 10-gallon fish tank often serves as an ideal home for a single Leopard gecko. This size fits in a small apartment, an office, or a young person's bedroom. And the habits of the Leopard gecko make tasks such as cage cleaning quick and easy.

Leopard geckos are the perfect pet size.

Chapter 3

Colors, Patterns, and Phases

Leopard geckos are extremely attractive animals. The average Leopard gecko is yellow with many black spots—hence its name. But the color patterns are extremely variable. This variability has enabled skilled breeders to create beautiful versions of the standard yellow with dark spots. Breeders have achieved some stunning results by selectively breeding geckos with similar patterns.

The Language of Variation

This chapter covers many of the various colors, patterns, and phases you may encounter in your search for a Leopard gecko. When discussing all these variations, the following terms are commonly used:

- **Color** is the base color of the lizard's skin.
- **Pattern** is the design created by the arrangement of the gecko's black spots.
- **Phase** (sometimes called morph) is the collection of selectively bred traits that affect a gecko's appearance.

Always keep marketing techniques in mind when you hear about a new phase of designer Leopard gecko. When sales are slow, some business-oriented breeders may release a new phase name, intending to increase interest in and sales of their animals. Use your judgment when evaluating a new phase. Sometimes it's a stretch of the imagination, and other times it is truly new and stunning. Surprises do crop up now and then, like the new albino Leopard gecko.

When choosing a designer gecko, always base your decision on your real feelings. If you like the way the gecko looks and appreciate his beauty, then you have found the gecko for you.

Albino or Amelanistic

An albino gecko is cream colored with pink eyes. Breeders have been hoping to attain this mutation for years, and recently several breeders have succeeded in producing albinos at generally the same time. Because there is usually a large interest among hobbyists in owning albino forms of reptiles, breeders expect that it will encourage the large-scale production of albino Leopard geckos.

The addition of this color will change the number of available phases in amazing ways over the next few years. Within a fairly short time you can expect to see albino stripes and, eventually, albino snow (see the explanation of the snow pattern on page 34) Leopard geckos, which would be patternless and pure white.

There is wide variation in the albino patterns currently being bred.

Variety Is the Spice of Domestic Life

The development of a wide variety of patterns and colors among Leopard geckos mirrors a long-established trend among keepers of many types of animals. Hobbyists have long manipulated the colors and other external characteristics of snakes, fish, birds, and mammals.

In fact, selective breeding is behind the domestication of all commercially important animals, including pigs, cattle, horses, and chickens. By selecting for traits such as calm temperament or high milk output, breeders seek to increase the animal's (or plant's) value and adaptability to captivity.

However, in considering animals that are technically "wild," such as reptiles and fish, we must take care never to release captive-bred individuals into any natural habitat. The genetic changes that occur as a result of selective breeding, while desirable in pets, may have disastrous consequences for free-living populations.

For example, farmed salmon are bred to be much larger than wild fish. However, a decrease in fertility accompanies the increased size. Farmed males who escape (a common occur-rence) generally mate with far more females than do wild males, because females use body size as the main factor in mate selection. The farmed males thus pass on the genes for decreased fertility—a factor that could, over time, have grave consequences for the entire species.

Albino Patternless or Amelanistic Patternless

An albino patternless gecko is cream colored with no trace of the spotting or banding of a regular albino. This phase was created by line breeding a patternless gecko with an albino.

The fewer the spots on a high yellow gecko, the higher the cost.

Circle Back

This gecko has a black circle, made up of connected spots similar to a bull's-eye, on his back. Julie Bergman, owner of the Gecko Ranch in northern California, noticed a nearly complete circle of connected dots during her gecko-breeding efforts and worked to eventually produce animals with a full circle.

High Yellow

This gecko has fewer spots than other Leopard geckos, on a bright yellow body. This phase can vary greatly among breeders. Some geckos will have fewer spots than others. High yellow has generally become the standard Leopard gecko. The fewer the spots, the higher the cost of the gecko.

Jungle

These geckos have black spots that connect in random patterns reminiscent of camouflage patterns, but using only yellow and black. The best examples of this phase are animals with large areas of bright yellow with very unusual, irregular patterns made up of black.

A variation of the basic jungle pattern, this one is called jungle chocolate.

The jungle phase may be the best for unusual designs, due to the connect-the-dots nature of the patterning. No two jungle phase Leopard geckos look alike. Breeders who look very closely and hold back unusual specimens for breeding can produce many unique designs.

Lavender Leopard

Leopard geckos tend to have a lavender tint in the white areas of their skin. Many generations of selective breeding have produced geckos with large and brighter areas of lavender.

Leusistic

True leusistic geckos are pure white with dark eyes. One breeder noticed this mutation and has started a breeding program. Due to Leopard geckos' fast maturation and prolific nature, these animals should be available within a short

This is a lavender baby.

time. The first offerings will be very expensive, but soon enough prices will drop considerably.

Melanistic

A melanistic gecko is almost completely black or very dark with little or no pattern showing. After years of developing brighter and lighter geckos, some breeders realized they could develop an all-black gecko by retaining darker animals over successive generations.

Many wild-caught Leopard geckos are naturally much darker than their commercially bred counterparts. Even the plainest of commonly bred geckos are brighter than many wild geckos. A few breeders have selected the darkest of these animals to breed. As yet unnamed, perhaps breeders will call them black panthers.

Patternless

Patternless geckos have an even yellow color with no spotting or banding. When these geckos are born, they are spotted and have dark pigmentation, but as they grow older they lose all patterns and are all yellow. Some are darker yellow; these geckos are in less demand.

This is a blizzard—pure white with red eyes.

The reverse stripe makes a striking pattern.

Dealers mistakenly applied the term "leusistic" to these geckos when they first became available, and some people continue to use the term. As word gets out that these lizards are truly a patternless phase, people will stop using the term "leusistic."

Reverse Stripe

The reverse stripe phase is the opposite of the striped phase: White stripes outline a dark stripe on either side, down the gecko's back to the tip of his tail.

Snow

These geckos have the normal color patterns, except they appear on a white background instead of a yellow one.

Striped

This attractive gecko has a lightly colored stripe running from the top of his head down his back to the tip of his tail. Thin black stripes outline this light stripe on both sides. A striped gecko can be difficult to find, because producing stripes can be tricky.

This striped gecko is still a baby.

Tangerine

These geckos have large areas of bright orange colors. The more orange pigmentation in the gecko, the more expensive he is. A breeder developed this phase after noticing a small area of orange on the rear legs of some geckos. Retaining these color areas and watching the outcome of breedings have led to increased orange pigmentation with each gen-

Orange is the desired color in tangerine geckos.

eration. These geckos have generated a great deal of excitement among keepers, and they are in high demand.

Part II

Caring for Your Leopard Gecko

Chapter 4

Choosing Your Leopard Gecko

Once you have decided the Leopard gecko is the right pet for you, you'll need to find one. Selecting the right Leopard gecko is important, so take your time and choose carefully. Think about all the colors and patterns ahead of time. Know the animal. Plan ahead and have a vivarium set up in advance (see chapter 5, "Housing Your Leopard Gecko"). Have food insects available as well (see chapter 6, "Feeding Your Leopard Gecko").

Where to Shop

Places for selecting your Leopard gecko range from your local pet store to local breeders and reptile expos to mail order from specialized breeders.

Herpetological Society Meetings

Local herpetological society meetings are great places to find Leopard geckos, plus you'll have a support network. Nearly every state has a herpetological society.

If you live in the vicinity of a herp society, you should attend meetings, and you will most likely find members who breed geckos and bring them to meetings for sale. At these meetings you will find a friendly atmosphere, with many knowledgeable society members ready to offer you information and moral support.

Join Your Local Herpetological Society

Enhance the educational value of your pet lizard by joining a local herpetological society. These groups will conduct seminars and provide literature on all aspects of lizard care. Other experienced lizard owners can share their tips with you. Older, well-established herpetological societies often have valuable ties with zoos, museums, and universities and may cooperate with them on research projects. Professional herpetologists associated with these institutions may make themselves available to society members for lectures or by offering advice and career guidance. Best of all, your herpetological society may work to ensure the safety of lizards in their natural environment. By getting involved, you can learn about lizards and help to protect them at the same time.

Pet Stores

Pet stores may be the easiest starting place for most people to find a pet gecko. Shopkeepers can order what you want if they do not have it in stock. The drawback is that unless you know and trust your local retailer, you have no idea where your Leopard gecko came from or if she is healthy.

Many pet stores order all their reptiles from a wholesaler. These animals may be wild caught, or dealers may have caged them with wild-caught animals. This is a very important concern: Even if the animal you want is captive bred, if she has been caged with wild-caught animals she may have been exposed to disease and parasites.

Also, because retailers have space limitations and the animals are usually in the store for a short period, pet stores sometimes house several species within the same display cage. One day a wild-caught gecko may be in a display cage, and the next day a captive-bred Leopard gecko is placed in the same cage. The wild-caught animal may have left something unhealthy behind. Busy pet stores don't always have the time to sterilize a cage between animals, which would prevent the transmission of diseases and parasites.

The selection of animals in a pet store will also be limited, and only one or two geckos may be available at a time. Being able to see a few different color phases may be important to you.

The best selection, offered by knowledgeable dealers, can be found at reptile shows.

Make sure that the retailer knows about the proper care of this species and will be able to answer your questions. Ask if the retailer has experience with the species or can put you in contact with the original breeder of the gecko. If you hear statements you know are not true, or are basically an attempt to sidestep your questions, take your business elsewhere.

Reptile Expos

If you want the absolute largest number of animals from which to choose, attend a reptile expo or herp show. At an expo you can see all the different color phases and ranges of geckos, and find the most competitive prices. Expos have become very common and are within driving distance of most major cities. Organizers most frequently hold them in late spring and early fall. In those months you will find the largest available number of geckos, because in cooler months most breeders hibernate their geckos.

To locate a herp show, check the listings in reptile magazines or on the Internet. At larger shows, such as the one held annually in Daytona Beach, Florida, you will see a startling variety of reptiles, amphibians, invertebrates, and plants. Many of these may be quite rare and not regularly exhibited in zoos. Government fish and wildlife agencies are usually present at these shows, so you are safe in assuming that the animals are legal to purchase.

Choosing a breeder to buy from can be as important as choosing the gecko. Look at the overall presentation of the breeder's animals and assess the breeder's willingness to talk about the animals and their care.

Most expos invite local herpetological societies. You can ask herp society volunteers to assist you in selecting an animal. Make sure the vendor from whom you decide to purchase an animal is willing to answer all your questions, can provide a history of the animal, and will be available after the sale. Finding a vendor who is willing to answer questions after you've taken your pet home is extremely important. Don't be afraid to ask.

The Ideal Age

When selecting a gecko, always ask how old the animal is. Do not purchase a very young hatchling; a gecko should be at least 6 weeks old when sold. At this age, the gecko will be able to handle the change of environment.

When you bring a gecko home, she will go through a natural period of adjustment. During this period she may not eat and may remain hidden; this is normal. Usually within a couple days she will relax and begin to adjust. However, when a hatchling is sold too young, she does not have any fat reserves and a period of fasting can be very detrimental.

Sometimes breeders ship animals to a wholesaler, who then ships them to a retailer. The process of shipping from breeder to wholesaler to retailer can be a fairly long period to go without food or water, especially for a hatchling. Some wholesalers may even cool down their stock so they do not have to feed or clean up after them. The hatchlings are not likely to arrive in the best condition.

If you want to breed geckos, avoid full-grown adults. Sometimes breeders will sell off old stock who can no longer produce eggs. These animals can make good pets, but without knowing their age, you will not know how long they have left to live. If you intend to breed your geckos and you buy an older animal, you may end up disappointed when she does not produce eggs.

A young animal is a better choice, especially if you plan to breed your geckos.

It is best to buy a juvenile Leopard gecko. They have adjusted to life. They are eating well and they have some size on them. At this stage they will still have their juvenile color patterns.

Buying a Leopard gecko at a young age is not essential, but it makes the process of raising a gecko fun. Watching them grow and change is one of the best parts of keeping this species. Raising a younger animal will also give you and the gecko a chance to get to know each other very well.

Re-grown Tails

Breeders may offer geckos with missing or re-grown tails at discounted prices. Buying a gecko in this condition may or may not be for you. There are reasons to avoid a gecko who is missing all or part of her tail.

The Leopard gecko, like many other species of gecko and lizard, can lose her tail rather easily. This loss can come from rough handling, accidents, or fighting with another gecko. If you're searching for a bargain, a Leopard gecko with a re-grown tail is a good opportunity. The re-grown tail will not look as nice as the original, but the loss of the original tail does not affect the animal's overall health.

This gecko has a re-grown tail. The new tail will usually be shorter than the old one.

Some large-scale dealers often buy huge numbers of geckos at one time and keep them in bins all together. This overcrowding results in tail nipping and possibly other injuries, such as missing toes or damaged skin. Breeders then sell these geckos at discounted prices.

It is best to avoid this type of dealer, but, with proper care, these geckos can recover and are usually inexpensive. Sometimes geckos drop their tails even with the best breeders, so do not consider a breeder inexperienced or unworthy if you see one offering these geckos for sale.

Detecting a Re-grown Tail

The original tail is segmented and textured, with a ringlike pattern at the tail tip. The re-grown tail will be smooth with no trace of the ringed texture. The overall scales will be finer, as well. The color and pattern of the tail can be similar to the original or completely different. Some will even be black.

The shape of the new tail can vary greatly. Most will be shorter than the original and usually very stout. Some are bulbous and rounded, while others may even be heart shaped. Occasionally you may see a tail with two distinct tips.

The location at which the tail breaks can affect the final shape. If the tail breaks near the tip, the re-grown tail will be very similar in shape to the original. Unless you look closely, you may not even notice much of a difference. The closer the break occurs to the body, the more bulbous the resulting new tail can be.

If Your Leopard Gecko Loses Her Tail

If your gecko loses her tail during her life with you, don't panic. The tail is designed to drop with minimal damage to the gecko. Special muscles cause the portion that is dropped off to wiggle and squirm. The reason for this adaptation is that, in the case of an attack from a predator, the motion of the tail will attract the predator's attention, allowing the gecko to escape. This method of escape is usually successful, and several types of lizards use it. Many wild-caught geckos have re-grown tails, so they must have had a close call at one time or another.

Once the tail is dropped, the part that remains attached to the gecko will immediately seal itself, because nearby blood vessels close quickly to prevent bleeding. Fluid and blood loss will be extremely minimal. Within a very short time the wound will show the beginnings of new tail growth. A small, pointed tail tip will emerge from the middle of the wound. This tip will steadily grow away from the body and thicken.

When You've Chosen Your Leopard Gecko

When you have selected a gecko, be prepared to ask the breeder or dealer some important questions before you finally decide to take your new pet home.

Assess Her Health

Look closely at each gecko before you select one. Try to look beyond her colors and pattern to assess her overall health. Look at the gecko's eyes. They should be bright and alert. Any sign that they are sunken indicates a dehydrated or sick animal. Any gecko kept in a cage with a sick gecko should be avoided. If one is sick, they may all be sick.

Look closely at the gecko's tail. It should be filled out and round. If the tail is flattened or has signs of the bones showing, avoid that gecko. She has not been fed enough, and sometimes these geckos do not recover. Look at where the tail joins the body. The hip area should be inspected closely. If there are any signs that the hipbones are protruding or showing, this is likely to be an under-fed animal.

Look closely at your gecko's overall condition before you decide to take her home.

Signs of Good Health

The gecko you choose should be in the best of health. Here's what to look for:

- Clear eyes (free of discharge)
- Clean nostrils (free of discharge)
- Closed, clean mouth
- Well-developed body (not bony)
- Good weight (hipbones not showing)
- Intact toes and claws (free of infection)
- Skin free of wounds, lumps, and discoloration
- Alert and active behavior

Verify Her Age

Ask how old the gecko is. About 6 weeks should be the minimum age; between 2 months and 1 year of age is perfect. At 1 year, Leopard geckos are essentially adults but will continue to grow a small amount. You will pay a higher price as the animal approaches 1 year of age, because at this stage you can probably use her for breeding.

Find Out How She Is Kept

Ask how the breeder is currently keeping the Leopard gecko. This information is not critical, because you may keep your gecko in any of the habitats described in chapter 5 ("Housing Your Leopard Gecko"), but it is good to know for your own peace of mind. Being prepared when you get home with your gecko will make everything much easier.

Also ask what they are feeding the gecko. Some breeders use a specific food item and your gecko may be used to that item. If you can have that type of insect ready, the period of adjustment will be easier on your pet.

> **T I P**
>
> It is best to have a vivarium completely set up before you shop for your gecko.

Environmental Ethics

We know surprisingly little about what constitutes a healthy, stable population of even the most common reptile species. What is known, however, is that many animals are rapidly declining in number. Perhaps the most frightening aspect of this situation is that some declines and even extinctions are apparently not attributable to traditional causes, such as habitat destruction, pollution, or overcollection. This state of affairs has led many scientists to speculate that less visible (and less preventable) factors, such as climate change, ozone layer depletion, or acid rain, may be at work. The disappearance of fragile life forms under these circumstances may indicate severe problems in the future for other species, ourselves included.

Every natural habitat develops to provide for all of its residents. For example, in a given environment, insects serve as food for reptiles and amphibians, which, in turn, serve as food for birds and small mammals. When a species is eliminated from the environment, or a species is introduced by humans, the natural balance of the habitat is disrupted. To do your part in maintaining the balance, leave wild animals in the wild and do not release pet species into a wild environment.

Given these facts, it should be clear that the removal of each individual animal from the wild is a significant event. Extinctions, most unnoticed, occur every day—each causing a degree of stress for other species and each closing the door on the medicinal value that the species may have had.

Captive Bred vs. Wild Caught

Breeders readily produce Leopard geckos in captivity. This fact is very important, for several reasons. In buying a captive-bred gecko you can be sure you have not contributed to the capture and removal of animals from their natural habitat. The wild areas of the world are shrinking, and many populations of wild animals are at risk. Mass collection for the pet trade can harm wild populations.

Gecko health is also at risk when you buy wild-caught animals. Geckos can sustain injuries from the collection process or from the hazards of living in the wild. Many wild-caught geckos will have scar tissue from healed injuries and re-grown tails.

Therefore, it is imperative that you avoid collecting wild animals and that you participate, if at all possible, in species conservation. Some ways in which you might brighten the future for Leopard geckos and other animals include the following:

• Consider turning your hobby into a career, so that your interest might benefit the entire species rather than just your collection. Investigate educational requirements and gain experience by volunteering at a zoo or a museum.
• Read widely and publish any observations that might be of use to others. The newsletters of local herpetological societies are excellent first-publication venues.
• Support and communicate with the research programs of zoos, museums, universities, and government organizations.
• Support environmentally sound legislation and political candidates who favor it.
• Volunteer your services to zoos, museums, and nature centers. Many are underfunded and welcome the assistance of serious hobbyists. They and local governmental agencies may sponsor release programs, surveys, rescue efforts, or field studies.
• Join herpetological societies and gecko interest groups, as well as the membership societies of zoos and museums.
• Above all, learn as much as you can, do not be afraid to approach professionals for advice, and share your observations, passion, and concern with others.

One very serious health issue is internal parasites (see chapter 7, "Keeping Your Leopard Gecko Healthy," for more information on this health problem). Wild-caught geckos frequently have internal parasites that require a veterinarian's care. Treatment and office visits can be expensive. For this reason alone, buying a captive-bred animal is often an exceptional bargain.

Wild-caught geckos require special care in acclimating to captivity, too. They will be less inclined to act as calm as captive-bred geckos.

Unsuspecting buyers who purchase wild-caught animals, unaware of the added care they require, may be sadly disappointed when their gecko does not thrive.

A Job for the Pros

There are some valid reasons for importing wild-caught animals. These animals are of great importance in starting captive populations and in adding genetic diversity to limited captive gene pools. However, these geckos should not be part of the retail pet trade.

Collecting geckos (or any animals) from the wild should only be carried out under the supervision of professional herpetologists associated with reputable zoos, museums, universities, or other scientific organizations. Such institutions may welcome the assistance of competent volunteers, so be sure to investigate these possibilities. Field research will enable you to contribute to conservation efforts in a very real way. For many, volunteer research programs become eye-opening experiences that start one down the path to a rewarding career in science or natural history.

Is This Gecko Wild Caught or Captive Bred?

Some uncaring retailers have been known to sell wild-caught geckos as captive bred, so be careful when selecting a retailer. When making a selection, it is always a good idea to ask if the gecko is captive bred. A complex network of international, national, and local laws govern reptile ownership, and the fact that an animal is offered for sale is not a guarantee of her legality. As purchaser, you are bound by all applicable laws, even if you are unaware of their existence, so please check carefully before buying a pet reptile.

There are several things to look for when you are trying to evaluate a gecko you suspect may be wild caught. Always be wary when you see a full-grown adult gecko for sale. Breeders sell most captive-bred geckos as juveniles or young adults, because it is expensive to raise a gecko to adult size for resale. Most buyers are not willing to pay the substantial extra cost for an adult captive-bred gecko. Remember, it takes almost a year for geckos to reach a mature size. During this time a breeder must feed and house these animals, and adult geckos require a great deal of space.

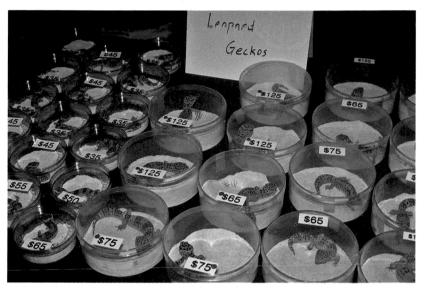

Make sure the gecko you buy is captive bred. It's the ethical choice, plus she'll make a better pet.

When first evaluating a gecko, look closely at the tail. If you see a re-grown tail, you should be cautious. Wild-caught Leopard geckos also tend to look generally darker and less colorful than most captive-bred geckos. They tend to have more spotting and duller yellows. They are also generally not as calm as captive-bred geckos.

The cost difference between captive-bred and wild-caught geckos is very minimal. In many cases, captive-bred animals cost about twice as much as the wild-caught version, but this should not be the case with Leopard geckos. Breeders have become very adept at providing quality animals at reasonable costs. Leopard geckos have become one of the most affordable reptile pets, although specialty designer geckos will cost substantially more due to the extremely careful selective breeding necessary to produce these beauties.

Chapter 5

Housing Your Leopard Gecko

Before you bring home your gecko, set up his housing and have all the supplies you need for your animal to thrive. Gecko housing can vary greatly, depending on your personal situation. Proper setups can include a visually pleasing vivarium with natural *substrate* (materials used to cushion the bottom of a vivarium) and plants, or a simple ventilated plastic sweater box with paper towels for substrate and a hide box.

The Vivarium

A naturalistic vivarium can be a very pleasing addition to your home. It becomes a visual centerpiece in any room. All-glass enclosures look clean and neat and are readily available. When the right materials fill them, they look like windows into another world. Leopard geckos do very well in these types of enclosures. Some reptiles are a challenge to keep in a natural setup, as they tend to be very active and can destroy the décor, but Leopard geckos are methodical in their movements and not prone to thrashing behavior.

A vivarium can be custom made out of wood that matches your furniture or made to fit in a room's unique space, such as an unused corner. Some cabinet-type designs are made to look like antiques or are especially sleek and easy to clean. A vivarium can also be made from a standard fish tank.

Keep in mind that Leopard geckos are nocturnal, so they will not typically be walking about during the day. They will need places to hide and feel safe. Natural vivariums have the advantage of looking great even when the inhabitants are hidden from view.

While an adult gecko can live quite happily in a 10-gallon aquarium or similarly sized sweater box, a 15- or 20-gallon tank is a better choice. A pair or trio should, ideally, be housed in at least a 29- or 30-gallon aquarium. Smaller enclosures can be made "larger" (from your pet's perspective) by using rocks and driftwood to create vertical space in the form of ledges and shelves.

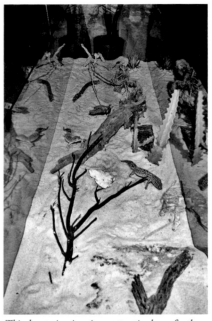

This desert vivarium is an attractive home for these two Leopard geckos.

Sand substrate, stacked rocks, cork bark, and a few plants can be fashioned into a stunning display. To prepare a 29-gallon fish tank for your geckos, you will need a few things (in addition to the aquarium, of course):

- Basking light
- Hide box
- Screen lid
- Substrate
- Water dish
- Thermometer

This list is for a basic setup that will work well. The screen lid should be all metal, rather than the plastic-framed type; the plastic frame can melt under a basking light.

Unlike many gecko species, Leopard geckos cannot climb glass. You should still use lid clamps (available at pet supply stores) to prevent your pets from escaping, just in case they reach the tank's top by scrambling up cage decorations such as rocks and logs. A securely fastened lid will also dissuade other pets and small children from becoming too "friendly" with your geckos.

Substrate

There are a number of substrates you can use in designing a Leopard gecko's home. Sand of various types is an obvious choice if you want to keep your desert-dwelling pets in a naturalistic vivarium. Unlike some reptile and amphibian species that commonly swallow sand when they eat, which can block the digestive tracts, Leopard geckos do quite well when kept on sand. Not only does the sand look nice, but it also seems to encourage natural walking and digging activities.

Aquarium gravel or small rocks, used alone or in combination with sand, are also suitable substrates and will add to your vivarium's natural appearance. Avoid sharp-edged gravel, which may cause problems if swallowed. You might also mix in some wood chips, orchid bark (the substrate potted orchids are grown in), or dead grass to simulate a semidesert habitat.

The substrate used within caves and other shelters should be orchid bark, sphagnum moss, or a similar material that retains moisture, to create an area of increased humidity for your pet.

Paper towels are the mainstay substrate of commercial breeders and hobbyists with large collections of lizards. Usually, they keep their animals in a simple sweater-box setup, and in this situation, paper towels are an excellent choice. They provide secure footing for your pet and, being fairly absorbent, help maintain cleanliness. Soiled towels can simply be discarded and replaced.

Wood chips, sand, or aquarium gravel make suitable substrates.

Lighting the Enclosure

Most lizards are active during the day and spend a good deal of time basking in the sun. In captivity, these species must be provided with ultraviolet A light to enhance their natural behavior and ultraviolet B light to enable them to synthesize vitamin D and absorb calcium. Leopard geckos, being nocturnal by nature, obtain vitamin D from their diet and do not need special ultraviolet light in captivity.

Still, they do need light. It will keep the plants in your vivarium healthy and will help simulate the day and night cycle. Even though nocturnal geckos do not bask, over-head lighting works well as a heat source, too, by imitating the way the sun works in nature. The overhead sun heats the ground and air, and at night, after sundown, the tempera-ture drops. Basking lights work the

> **CAUTION**
>
> Do not leave the basking light on all night—your nocturnal lizard needs time in the dark.

same way. They have the added benefit of being very inexpensive and reliable, and they can be simple to operate.

You should place a basking light on one side of the cage, so that your gecko can choose where he is most comfortable. Bear in mind that while your geckos may not actually come out and bask under the light, they may seek out the residual heat that has built up in the substrate directly below the light, even after it has been turned off. The side with the basking light will be warm, and the opposite end should be considerably cooler. Be aware that animals will often choose security over optimal temperature. If your Leopard gecko feels cool, he can move to the warmer side. If he is particularly shy, you may need to position hide boxes on both the warm and cool sides of the vivarium.

Light just one side of the vivarium, so your pet can get away from the light and the heat it generates.

Beware of Hot Rocks

Hot rocks (fake rocks with heating elements inside) are found in pet supply stores and are designed to provide reptiles with a simple way to thermoregulate. Unfortunately, lizards and snakes don't always know when they should move away from a hot rock and have been known to badly burn themselves. This occurs most commonly with pets who use the rocks when air temperatures are fairly cool. Although the phenomenon is not completely understood, it seems that the cool air from above signals the animal to remain on the rock, even while the creature's ventral surface is becoming dangerously hot. Other heat sources are readily available and are much safer for your pet.

An ordinary household incandescent bulb will work as a basking light; you need not buy an expensive reptile bulb, because Leopard geckos do not require full-spectrum lighting. The wattage needed depends on the size of the tank and the temperature of the room it's in. For a 29-gallon tank in a 70°F (21°C) room, a 40- to 60-watt bulb is usually enough to warm the side of the tank near the bulb to about 85°F (29°C) and the cooler side to about 75°F (24°C). That's just the way your gecko likes it during the day. At night it is safe for the temperature in the vivarium to drop to 68°F to 72°F (20°C to 22°C). If your home is unusually cold at night, you may need a heat mat (see page 55) to maintain the minimum temperature.

Timing your enclosure's overhead lighting can affect the animals' activity periods. You can set a timer so the basking lights turn off at dinner time or in the evening, when you have time to enjoy watching your geckos. When the basking lights are off, Leopard geckos will begin to become active even if your home lights are still on.

This is a good time to offer your gecko food, because you will be able to watch him in action. Watching a Leopard gecko slowly stalk an insect can be an amazing sight.

You can also get light bulbs designed specifically for viewing nocturnal pets. These will enable you to easily observe behaviors that might otherwise be largely hidden from you, and will greatly enhance the overall experience of owning a gecko.

Keeping It Warm

An alternative way to heat your vivarium is with undertank heat mats. These mats are placed under the bottom of the tank and provide a warm area for your geckos. Like basking lights, place the mats on one side of the tank so that a cooler area is available.

Heat mats do not heat the air temperature of the cage, but create local warm spots. You should use a thermostat with these units so the mat does not become too hot. Some units contain built-in thermostats. Make sure you place a thermometer on the substrate to check the temperature, even if you have a thermostat.

Whichever heating method you choose, make a habit of regularly checking temperatures within the vivarium. Placing two thermometers in the vivarium is a really good idea, so you can check the temperature in the warm side and the cool side. Place one thermometer right under the basking bulb or right over the heat mat. The other should be placed on the substrate at the cool end. Knowing the temperatures in these areas will enable you to adjust the heat according to the surrounding temperatures in your home.

In hot summer months, if your home is not air-conditioned, the hot temperatures may force you to turn off basking lights.

Creating Tunnels and Caves

You can design your gecko's hiding areas to be up against a viewing surface; a cave that uses the glass aquarium walls as part of its structure will give you a view of

your animals while they sleep. A series of tunnels can even be constructed against the front glass. You can make this type of cave or tunnel using materials from a local art supply store's sculpture department. There are several materials available that are very much like plaster. Dyes are also available to match your substrate.

If you press sand into the surface of these materials while they are still soft, the sand will adhere, making your cave or tunnel look even more natural. You can create very realistic surfaces using this technique. The same plaster-type material can be

Your gecko absolutely needs a place to hide.

TIP

Be sure to make a removable roof on all your caves and tunnels, or set up another way to clear feces and dead food insects from within the structures you construct.

spread over the back wall of the vivarium to create the look of a sandstone cliff. You can make the area uneven and mold ledges. This sort of formation will allow your geckos to explore and climb.

In addition to creating ledges, you can make depressions in the ledges and outcrops for small plants. Succulent plants can be the finishing touch that really makes the habitat look complete. (See "Adding Plants" on page 57 for more information on safe plants for your vivarium.)

Hiding Your Gecko's Hide Boxes

Specially designed lizard hide boxes and caves are available in pet supply stores. But you can also make hide boxes from plastic food storage containers. Quart-size containers are ideal for a single gecko. Cut a circular silver-dollar-size hole in one side to give the gecko access to the box. Make the hole up high on the side so that the substrate doesn't get kicked out of the box while the gecko digs. Inside, the box should be about half filled with a medium, such as damp sphagnum moss, that allows for increased humidity.

Even a plastic hide box can be part of a natural-looking enclosure. You can easily conceal hide boxes behind rocks or bark to give the illusion of a natural habitat, while ensuring that your animals have what they need to feel secure.

Placing the hide box toward the back of the vivarium is usually the easiest solution. Then you can build rockwork around it or even slide it into a cave you have made out of sculpting materials. This way, when you need to remove the box for maintenance, you can easily slip it in or out with minimal disturbance of the décor. You will need to remove the box frequently during the breeding season to remove eggs, and also for regular cleaning.

Humidity

While Leopard geckos come from dry areas, they spend a great deal of time below ground, where there is moisture. The increased humidity is very important when they are shedding. Without proper humidity, it would be difficult for the gecko to complete the shedding process.

Retained patches of unshed skin can lead to *necrosis* of the underlying layer of skin—the skin that is covered by unshed layers turns black and becomes infected. Toes can suffer greatly from incompletely shed skin. The unshed skin is

The plastic container is filled with damp moss, so these geckos will have the humidity they need.

like a glove that is too tight. This skin cuts off circulation and the affected toe will die and fall off, which can lead to a fatal infection. The humidity levels in the air can also affect long-term respiratory health.

An ideal way to maintain the humidity your pet needs is to provide a hide box filled with damp sphagnum moss in one corner of his home.

Adding Plants

The décor in your gecko's vivarium can include succulent plants that thrive in dry environments, rocks, driftwood, cork bark, or dried cholla wood. You can plant many species of succulents, as long as they do not have spines or thorns. Haworthia and aloe both work very well. The South African succulents called living stones are a very nice, subtle addition to your vivarium.

Some succulents, such as euphorbias, while thornless, may exude a toxic sap. Avoid these types of plants. Leopard geckos will not eat them, but crickets might. If a cricket eats the plant and then the Leopard gecko eats the cricket, you may be in for trouble.

Also avoid any spiny plants such as cacti. Even though Leopard geckos come from a desert environment, a cactus invites the chance of an injury.

If you have a rock or gravel substrate, just leave the plants in their pots and sink the pots into the substrate. If you have a sand substrate, bear in mind that

Understanding and Avoiding Salmonella

Salmonella is a type of bacteria that is often associated in people's minds with reptiles. In fact, Salmonella is extremely common on nearly all surfaces, and most of us come in contact with a good deal of it each day. Salmonella is frequently found on eggshells and chicken skin, a fact that accounts for the frequency of outbreaks following picnics, where unrefrigerated and undercooked foods are often consumed. While we should assume that all reptile pets harbor it on their skin and, often, within their digestive tracts, Salmonella is also commonly found in pets such as dogs and cats.

This resilient pest also survives well on inanimate surfaces. Not long ago, many people who had visited the Denver Zoo in Colorado were taken ill and diagnosed with Salmonella. The strain of the bacteria was identical to that cultured from the surface of the public railing in front of the Komodo dragon exhibit. Each affected visitor was found to have leaned on the railing and later to have eaten "finger foods" such as pizza. Apparently, the keepers servicing the Komodo dragon exhibit had transferred Salmonella from their hands to the railing, and the visitors had not washed properly (or at all!) before eating.

Salmonella can be found in a great variety of strains, or types, some of which are quite virulent and capable of causing severe illness or even death. The risk is particularly acute for people whose immune systems

many live plants do not do well in pure sand, so you may wish to leave these in their pots as well. If you wish to plant directly into sand, mix some potting soil into the area where you want to plant (use a type specifically designed for succulents) and choose hardy, desert-dwelling plants.

Surprisingly, a heavily planted tank with numerous caves and hiding spots will result in more, not less, viewing opportunities, and will enable you to see a great deal of natural behavior. The reason for this is that your pet will feel safer and therefore more confident moving around such a home than he would in a more sterile setup.

If you choose to include living plants in your enclosure, be sure to add proper lighting. Many of these plants require high levels of light. Full-spectrum fluorescent lamps often do the job. It is best to avoid placing any vivarium near a have been weakened by illness or compromised by disease, and for young children and elderly persons. Pet keepers living with such individuals should consult a health professional about the risks involved and for situation-specific advice.

You may wish to consult your doctor about the specific symptoms of Salmonella infection, and, in any event, it is prudent to let them know that you keep reptile pets.

Healthy reptile and amphibian pets are rarely bothered by normally occurring populations of Salmonella, but may become ill when other factors, such as disease or stress, are present.

Adults in good health can avoid contracting Salmonella by following these simple precautions:

- Wash your hands both before (so as not to transfer Salmonella *to* the lizard) and after handling your pet, whether you are planning to eat directly afterward or not.
- Implements and bowls used in your lizard's tank should *never* be used for any other purpose and should *never* be cleaned in a sink that is used to prepare your food. Clean such items in your bathroom, and scour the sink thoroughly afterward with an antibacterial preparation and paper towels.
- Never kiss your lizard—or any other pet, for that matter. (I know, this notion is quite shocking to many, especially to some dog owners!) This practice puts you at high risk for a Salmonella infection and also for a nasty bite. Bites to the lip area are quite painful, even from the smallest pets, and tend to leave permanent scars.

window that is exposed to direct sunshine. Direct sunlight shining in on a glass enclosure can quickly overheat and kill your gecko.

Adding Rocks

When stacking rocks in your Leopard gecko's vivarium, be sure to secure them in place. Gluing them together is a good way to prevent an accident from occurring. If rocks were to fall or a cave collapse, your animals could be severely injured or killed.

Epoxy or silicone works well as an adhesive. Both are very strong, readily available, and easy to use. They do require a curing time before they are fully set and stop exuding fumes. Carefully follow the product instructions before placing the rocks in with your animals. The fumes that are exuded during the curing

Make sure the rocks you add do not have sharp edges and are carefully secured in the vivarium.

process can be harmful to you and your geckos, so make sure the curing process occurs in a well-ventilated area. Once the product has cured, the rocks are inert, safe, and long lasting.

Be careful when placing flat rocks on a substrate such as sand. Geckos can burrow under rocks, causing them to collapse or fall, trapping or crushing the unfortunate animals in the process. Gluing small supports under a flat rock solves this problem. This creates a tablelike structure that will support the rock if the gecko's digging removes the underlying sand. You can also place heavy rocks directly on the bottom of the tank and build the substrate up around them.

Building a Custom Habitat

If you are handy or have a friend who is, you can build a habitat to suit your own design or home. The possibilities are endless. You can use wood that matches your furnishings. You can create caves and tunnels that are exposed to the front glass. This exposure enables you to see your geckos while they are in their burrows, which is very rewarding if you want to see Leopard geckos during the day.

Safety for your geckos is the prime concern when designing an enclosure. Be sure to use only appropriate materials and keep all edges smooth. If you use wood, seal it with a nontoxic material.

If you use any silicone sealants, make sure they are properly aged before adding animals to the cage. Silicone will emit toxic fumes while curing, and these can be dangerous to humans as well as to animals.

Make sure you glue all stacked rocks in place, because digging geckos can make a pile of seemingly stable rocks tumble. Ensure that all basking lights are out of reach of your geckos. A cold gecko who wants to warm up may get too close and get burned. Test all heating elements to be sure they do not get too hot.

Any custom cage should meet the basic needs of the geckos. Include hiding areas and enough surface area so that the geckos have ample room to move about and behave normally. All caging should have a secure top, as well, to keep out danger and to keep your geckos in the cage.

This homemade vivarium makes a nice home for a pair of geckos.

Cleaning Your Leopard Gecko's Habitat

Vivarium cleanup is fast and easy. Leopard geckos are creatures of habit and tend to defecate in the same location. Their stools are dry and very easy to collect. Urine is not voided separately, but rather is excreted in the form of dry white urates along with the feces.

If you spot clean the vivarium once or twice a week, the habitat will not develop an odor. An old spoon or a plastic spoon can be kept on hand to scoop out feces. Be sure to remove any insects that may have eluded your pet and subsequently died.

Water and food bowls should be cleaned with commercial dish soap and rinsed well. Be sure you do this in a bathroom or other sink that is not used for preparing your food, and wash the area well afterward (see "Understanding and Avoiding Salmonella," page 58).

It is a good idea to check the hide spots once a week, and to spray the substrate within with water as it dries out. You should also check the substrate, and in various rock crevices, for feces and dead insects that might otherwise escape your notice.

The vivarium glass can be cleaned, inside and out, with water and paper towels, or a solution of 20 percent vinegar in water if there are stains.

You will also need to top off the substrate from time to time, as a bit will likely be removed with the feces and dead insects.

Plant care will vary, depending upon the species you choose. Most succulents and desert plants require a weekly watering at most, with drier periods from

Leopard Geckos and Other Pets

If you have other pets, such as a cat, a dog, or a parrot, you need to think about keeping your Leopard gecko safe from them. Do not allow your pets to have unsupervised access to your gecko's enclosure. A cat or a dog with strong predatory instincts, or a large parrot, can make short work of a gecko. Even if your cat or dog doesn't outwardly harm the gecko, constant harassment can result in a fatal dose of stress for your lizard.

time to time. Be sure to research each type of plant carefully, and to incorporate its care into your basic routine.

Vivariums with deep sand substrates will rarely need to be broken down and washed (unless there has been an incidence of disease), especially if you maintain a regular routine of spot cleaning. If you are keeping your pets in plastic sweater boxes lined with paper towels, the paper towels must be replaced daily and the boxes will need to be washed out each week or so. A 20 percent bleach solution works well. Be sure to rinse and dry the containers thoroughly after washing.

Your geckos will not be particular about where they climb in their vivarium. To keep your pet healthy, make sure everything in his enclosure is clean.

Chapter 6

Feeding Your Leopard Gecko

Leopard geckos remain under rocks or in holes during the day and become active at dusk. In your vivarium they will have a similar rhythm of activity. Therefore, dusk is the best time to offer your pet food.

You can set the basking lights in your gecko's vivarium on a timer, so the lights turn off in the early evening. As soon as the lights go off your gecko will begin his activity period. Even with your room's overhead lights on, as long as the lighting is not extremely bright, it will appear to be dusk to your geckos.

As the geckos become active, you can sit back and watch them interact, eat, and explore. It is amazing how purposefully they will act. Hungry geckos will immediately perk up when they detect an insect. Many will raise themselves up high to have a better look and then slowly approach their prey. The tail movements during the stalking process are amazingly feline. The slow serpentine movement of the tail, while the gecko's body is motionless, can be hypnotic.

What to Feed

In the wild, Leopard geckos eat a wide variety of live insects and invertebrates such as spiders, as well as the occasional small mouse, lizard, or snake. For optimum health, a captive Leopard gecko's diet should include a variety of insects.

The food items that are generally commercially available are

- Crickets
- Mealworms
- Superworms (also called super mealworms)

No Need for Mice

Once in a while keepers feed their geckos baby mice (known in the trade as "pink mice" or "pinkies"), mostly to fatten breeding females. Great care should be taken when using pink mice as a food item. The Leopard gecko's digestive system is primarily designed to handle invertebrates, and it is likely that they only rarely consume small mammals in the wild.

Insectivorous reptiles and amphibians commonly develop eye problems and fat deposits around several internal organs when fed a diet that is high in pink mice and other vertebrates. This phenomenon has also been observed in widely different species in captivity, including White's tree frogs, Tiger salamanders, and Basilisks.

If you offer pinkies at all (and your Leopard gecko does not need them), feed them only to breeding females, and then feed only one mouse every other month or so.

- Waxworms
- Butterworms
- Silkworms
- Locusts
- "Feeder" lizards such as Anoles

How to Feed

There are several ways to offer insects to your gecko. Some keepers drop several crickets into the habitat at a regular time on designated nights. Others use feeding bowls and have food available at all times.

One advantage of dropping in food at a given time is that you are able to watch your lizard hunt her prey. The disadvantage is that any escaping insects could hide and remain in the cage for a very long time. Usually an insect lingering in your gecko's environment is a minor issue, but it can lead to problems.

Feeding live insects at designated meal times will enable you to watch your pet hunt.

Crickets, in particular, are very resourceful and perpetually hungry insects. Those that escape to an inaccessible hiding area may later find your sleeping gecko and begin to feed on it. These bites can lead to infection and can be dangerous. Also, bear in mind that the incessant chirping of male crickets can be maddening!

Another concern is that a hiding cricket will lose its nutritional value because it is not eating. Any supplement powder coating on the insects will quickly wear off (see page 67 for more on supplements). While hiding, a cricket may die and decay.

If you suspect that a cricket is hiding in your gecko's habitat, you can leave a small piece of carrot or apple for it to eat. The food tempts the cricket from its hiding spot, and the cricket will leave your gecko alone because it is busy eating. Once the cricket is out of its hiding spot, your gecko will most likely eat it.

Feeding bowls can make feeding an easy task. It is best to use very smooth bowls that do not allow insects a good foothold to climb. The insects remain in the bowl for the gecko to find whenever she is hungry. The depth and size of the bowl will vary with the type of insect you offer your gecko. Adding a small amount of powdered vitamin and mineral supplement to the bowl will ensure the insects retain their nutritional value.

It's best to offer larval feeder insects in bowls; mealworms and superworms are unable to escape from most feeding bowls. Crickets will need a slightly deeper bowl, and you may need to remove their rear legs to prevent escape. (A slight pinch to the base of the leg will cause the cricket to shed the leg, apparently with little if any distress.)

To make sure the insects remain nutritious while in the feeding bowl, keep small pieces of food in the bowl with them at all times. Cut vegetables, such as carrots, work well.

How Much Food?

In terms of frequency and quantity, there are several equally effective ways of feeding your pet. Newly hatched and juvenile geckos need the most nutrition and should be fed every day. Youngsters such as these can be fed as much as they care to eat. Dietary variety and vitamin-mineral supplementation (see page 67 for more on supplements) is particularly important at this time. Be on the lookout for smaller babies who are not getting their fair share of the food, and be sure to move them to separate quarters so they can eat and grow.

After the age of 6 to 8 months, you can reduce the frequency to three meals per week. If you prefer to feed your geckos more frequently (and many pet owners do!), simply reduce the amount of food offered at each meal. If you do, you can feed your pet every day—or almost every day.

An average-size meal for an adult gecko eating three times a week would be approximately three to four crickets, two to three superworms, or three to four waxworms. Eventually, you will see a predictable pattern in how much your gecko likes to eat (some seem to need more food than others), and you can adjust the amount to fit her individual metabolism, life stage, and or weight gain or loss.

TIP

When feeding Leopard geckos, a meal of several small insects is generally preferable to one of fewer large insects. Adult crickets, in particular, contain a proportionally larger percentage of indigestible body parts, such as wings and legs, than do immature individuals.

Well-fed geckos store a substantial amount of fat in their tail, so don't be shy about experimenting with dietary changes. If your own schedule demands it, you can reduce the number of weekly feedings while increasing the amount of food given each time. However, one large weekly meal, which is how reptiles such as snakes are fed, is not the healthiest way of feeding geckos or most other lizards.

Because geckos store up plenty of fat in their tail, you can experiment with how much you feed your gecko, and when.

Vitamins and Minerals

Nutritional supplements are very important when keeping captive reptiles, including Leopard geckos. Adding vitamins and minerals to a gecko's diet is very easy, and commercial supplements are readily available.

Minerals

Minerals are among the most vital food supplements, and calcium is the most important mineral supplement. Growing geckos need a regular supply of calcium if they are to have strong bones and grow properly. Breeding females need a regular supply of calcium so that they will develop eggs without depleting their body stores. Gravid (pregnant) females who are fed a calcium-poor diet will draw the mineral from their own bones. Unfortunately, calcium deficiencies are common, but they can be avoided.

You can add calcium to your gecko's diet by coating insects with a supplement before you feed them to your lizard. It is difficult to accurately recommend how often to feed coated insects to your gecko. The most common schedule is to coat every feeding for babies (except the day vitamin supplements are given), growing juveniles, and breeding females. For all other Leopard geckos, once a week is probably fine.

Geckos cannot live by worms alone. They need a calcium supplement.

Many breeders and experienced keepers will also leave a small dish of calcium powder in the vivarium at all times. Pet supply stores sell several brands, any of which will fill your gecko's need. A Leopard gecko will lick this powder whenever she feels she needs more calcium.

If Leopard geckos do not get enough calcium from the coated insects, they may eat the substrate in their vivarium. In the wild, eating calcium-rich sand can enrich their diet, but the sand in most vivariums is silica, which does not contain any calcium. Ingesting this sand substrate can block the digestive tract. For this reason, some breeders recommend that sand not be used as substrate.

This advice against sand is sound, but with proper calcium supplementation it is safe to use sand as a substrate. There are even commercial sands made from calcium carbonate. Ingesting these sands is safe and will actually provide the calcium the gecko is craving. However, these sands are expensive and their benefit has not been proven.

Vitamins

The action of vitamins in reptiles, and what their requirements are, is not well known. We know that some fat-soluble vitamins can be a problem in large doses. However, geckos need some of these vitamins for basic life functions, and deficiencies can be life threatening.

Use vitamin supplements carefully. You should offer them, but not as often as you give your pet mineral supplements. Once a week is probably more than enough for a good diet, but not enough to cause a problem.

Coat feeder insects with a vitamin powder on a day other than the one you coat them with mineral powder, because some minerals and vitamins interfere with one another and block absorption.

You should also investigate the combined vitamin and mineral supplements that are offered by reputable companies and specifically formulated for pet reptiles. A good deal of effort is being put into developing new products that may eliminate the need for separate vitamin-mineral supplementation. Reading articles published in reptile hobbyist magazines is a good way to evaluate the value of new products.

Most calcium supplements come with added vitamin D_3, which is necessary for absorption of calcium. The exact amounts of vitamin D_3 that your Leopard gecko needs are not known, but geckos seem to do well with a fairly low amount. Most of the commercial brands of calcium supplements provide a safe amount of this vitamin.

> **TIP**
>
> Insects tend to have high phosphorus levels; keeping the proper balance of calcium to phosphorus when supplementing can be tricky. Buying a calcium supplement that contains no phosphorus is best.

Dusting crickets with a vitamin and mineral supplement will help keep your gecko healthy.

How to Keep and Gut Load Crickets

Gut loading is the practice of supplying crickets with a nutritious diet so that the insects become healthy meals for the animals who consume them. The species that is most commonly bred as pet food and fishing bait is the house cricket, *Acheta domestica.*

To gut load crickets, you'll need to keep them for at least twenty-four hours (and preferably forty-eight) before you feed them to your lizard. Place the crickets in a plastic container with holes punched in the lid for air. An old margarine tub will do, or you can buy one of the commercial cricket containers available at pet supply stores. Give the crickets food and a crumpled-up paper towel or a section of egg carton in which to hide. Let them feast for at least an entire day before feeding them to your gecko.

Feeding crickets is not as hard as it sounds. Simply provide them with tropical fish food flakes (into which has been mixed a few pinches of vitamin-mineral supplement) and a variety of cut-up fruits and vegetables (oranges, yams, carrots, apples, bok choy, grapes, dandelion greens, and a host of others are all readily consumed). Or you can buy commercially made cricket food, which is high in vitamins and minerals, at your pet supply store (the fruits and vegetables are still necessary). Crickets that consume a healthy, varied diet will pass on important nutrients to your gecko.

Crickets require water for drinking, but possess the suicidal impulse to drown themselves in even the smallest amount of standing water. Water can be provided in bowls filled with wet cotton or via specially designed "cricket drinkers." However, the easiest way is to keep the crickets supplied with fresh fruits and vegetables. This ensures a safe supply of water (contained in the produce) and carries with it the added bonus of increasing the crickets' nutritional value.

While they do require a source of drinking water, house crickets cannot tolerate damp environmental conditions and will quickly sicken and die if not kept fairly dry.

Crickets may be kept at normal room temperatures. Insect metabolisms quicken as temperatures rise, so be sure to provide the crickets with extra food, water, and ventilation if they are kept in warm areas. Bear in mind that even a small number of males can be quite noisy.

Mealworms and super mealworms will consume the same foods, along with oatmeal and dry baby pablum mix.

How to Coat Feeder Insects

Coating feeder insects with a supplement is easy. You just shake the insects in a container with a small amount of the powder supplement. You can use a plastic bag, a paper cup, or a special commercial container.

The commercial coating device will probably find its way into many keepers' basic supplies. After coating the insects, you flip the container upside down to sift the excess powder from the insects. Sifting excess powder enables you to reuse the powder and to offer insects without dust drifting through the air. The fine dust in a vivarium, when breathed into the lungs, can be an irritant.

Wild-Caught Invertebrates

Wild geckos likely consume a wide variety of insects and other invertebrates, thus ensuring a balanced diet. Captive animals, however, are generally kept on diets that are limited to the few insects that are bred commercially. Vitamin and mineral supplementation is one way to address this situation, but the state of our knowledge in this area leaves much to be desired.

You can add much-needed variety to your pet's diet by feeding her wild-caught insects and other invertebrates. Moths, grasshoppers, sow bugs, beetles, small spiders, caterpillars, and scores of other such creatures will be relished by your geckos. The vigor of their reaction when presented with these new foods will leave no doubt in your mind as to their appreciation of your efforts.

The term *meadow plankton* refers to the myriad invertebrates that may be easily collected by sweeping a net through tall grass, even in the heart of the busiest cities. When using this and other collection methods, you must be certain that you can distinguish potentially dangerous types, such as bees, wasps, and certain spiders, from the more palatable ones. Under no circumstances should you handle any insect that you cannot

In the wild, Leopard geckos eat a wide variety of insects and other invertebrates. You can improve the variety in your pet's diet by going out and hunting for her.

identify, due to the possibility of severe or even fatal stings, or dangerous allergic reactions to stings and bites.

When feeding tiny geckos, you can place the collected grass and meadow plankton into a container that is perforated so that only the smaller insects will be able to get out and enter the vivarium.

Commercially made light, baited, or hormone-infused traps are available to help control common garden pests such as gypsy moths. Most keep the insects alive for later collection. Boards, rocks, and tarps placed on the ground will attract a variety of invertebrates, as will cans buried flush with the ground and baited with banana or fish. Perhaps the most enjoyable way of obtaining invertebrates is to simply turn over rocks and logs as you walk about. Be sure to replace such structures carefully, and always check local regulations before collecting.

While I have not personally encountered a case of secondary insecticide poisoning (the gecko is poisoned after eating an insect that has consumed or been coated with insecticide) as a result of using wild-caught invertebrates, it would be prudent to avoid collecting in areas that are known to be treated with insecticides. Always reject insects that are obviously sick or otherwise in distress.

Water

Provide your gecko with a shallow dish of water. This is usually the best way to give a Leopard gecko the moisture she requires. Some breeders have a water dish available at all times and others offer the dish twice a week. Either way is fine as long as you do not leave your geckos without water for more than a few days at a time or forget to clean the dish.

There are many suitable types of containers that you can use as water dishes. Many reptile-industry manufacturers even make bowls that look like rock shallows and come in many colors to match your vivarium.

Whatever container you choose, it must meet several important criteria. The edge of the dish should not be too high. If the edge of the dish is higher than the gecko's head, your gecko may not notice the water. Shallow, flat-bottomed glassware about one-half to three-quarters of an inch high is perfect. The flat bottom keeps the dish stable so it will not tip over.

One of the biggest problems with water dishes is that they often trap crickets and other insects in the water, drowning them. This wastes the insects and fouls the water. You can easily avoid this problem by placing a stone in the water, so crickets can climb out of the dish. Place the stone near the bowl's edge.

Leopard geckos come from arid habitats, and in the wild may not often encounter standing water. They likely obtain drinking water by licking the dew from plants and other surfaces. If your gecko seems uninterested in a water

Keep the water bowl clean and make sure it's shallow enough for your gecko to climb out.

bowl, simply spray the glass, plants, and rocks in the vivarium with a fine mist of clean water once each day.

Keeping Your Gecko's Water Bowl Clean

Be sure to remove the bowl and thoroughly clean it every day to help prevent bacteria and fungus from growing in the water. To clean it, you can use a mild bleach and water mixture of one part bleach to thirty parts water. Be sure to rinse the bowl very well. Always clean water and food bowls and other objects from the vivarium in a bathroom or a utility sink, as opposed to a kitchen sink, so they do not come in contact with areas where you prepare food. The sink and surrounding area should be thoroughly disinfected afterward, as well.

There are also several commercial cleaning products specifically made for sanitizing reptile habitats and furnishings. These products all work well and are readily available from your local pet supply store.

Chapter 7

Keeping Your Leopard Gecko Healthy

Leopard geckos can live very long lives. There are records of individuals still going strong after 25 years. Good nutrition, proper housing and temperature, and a good environment all contribute to the well being of your gecko. Preventing maladies is always easier than curing them. But despite your best care, health problems can still arise. In this chapter, I'll review some of the most common ones.

Choosing a Veterinarian

It is best to pick out a veterinarian *before* you have a medical emergency. When considering prospective vets in your area, you should ask them if they have experience with reptiles. If they say yes, then ask if they have experience with geckos or other lizards.

Finding a good veterinarian for your Leopard gecko may be one of your most difficult tasks. While most vets are well trained in small animal care, only a few have had any training in the unique medical requirements of reptiles and amphibians. As a result, many veterinarians will refuse to examine your lizard.

The situation is improving, though. The number of people with pet reptiles has steadily increased, and many veterinary practices now include reptile care in their exotics departments. You can find veterinarians who are qualified to work with reptiles by calling your local herpetological society or by searching online (see the appendix).

Another choice, if you have a local wildlife rehabilitation center or zoo nearby, is to ask for their help. They might be able to point you to a good herp vet. The final option is to call any veterinarian in the phone book and ask for a recommendation to a good reptile veterinarian.

If you cannot find a reptile veterinarian in your area, consider using a veterinarian nearby and having them call in consultations to a reptile specialist.

Common Health Problems

When keeping animals, it is important to bear in mind that it is always in the animal's best interest to appear healthy. Even captive-born geckos will try to mask outward signs of illness, because sick-looking animals are singled out by predators looking for an easy meal. In other words, your lizard may appear healthy when he's not. This strategy is useful in the wild, but it complicates captive care. Often, the result is that you don't notice a problem until it is well advanced and therefore more difficult to treat.

It is, therefore, imperative that you understand your pet's normal behavior and recognize deviations from it. Even slight nuances of posture may be an important sign. Note how your lizard holds himself when moving about and resting, and also be aware of his general activity patterns. Perform a careful physical examination of your gecko if you note anything unusual.

If you are at all worried, take your gecko to the veterinarian. It's never foolish to bring your pet in to be checked. While a visit to a veterinarian can be expensive, responsible health care for your gecko is part of your commitment as caretaker. Home care is often ineffective and geckos die as a result.

Fortunately, Leopard geckos are hardy, and illness and injuries are

Get to know what's normal for your pet and you will be quick to notice when he's not feeling well.

Stress Can Be Deadly

It is important to understand the role of stress when considering the health of your pet and how to treat his ailments.
Stressed animals are prone to attack by microorganisms that
they might normally ward off. Large numbers of fungi, bacteria,
viruses, and the like are always present in the environment,
many of which cause no problems until the animal's immune
system is compromised.

In response to a threat or other stress, animals of all types
(ourselves included) release a host of biochemicals designed to
facilitate defense or escape. This is a quite necessary reaction
to danger. However, long-term exposure to these natural
chemicals weakens the immune system, leaving the animal vulnerable to parasites and disease. Because potential disease
vectors are always present in the environment, it is important to
provide your pet with a stress-free home.

Common stressors include improperly designed vivariums,
inappropriate temperatures, outside disturbances from people,
noise, or pets, aggressive tank-mates, and a poor diet. Factors
such as an improper diet are often long-term, and their effects
may become apparent only very gradually. The problems they
cause are therefore difficult to detect and cure.

not common. Keep your pet's habitat clean, feed and water him properly, and
keep the temperatures within normal range, and you will encounter few problems.

Digestive Tract Obstruction

One of the most frequent problems in Leopard geckos is a digestive tract
obstruction, which occurs when a gecko eats something indigestible. This indigestible object forms a blockage that can be fatal. It can be bark, gravel, or sand
that the gecko unintentionally consumed while seizing a prey insect, or it can be
substrate that the gecko intentionally ingested.

Animals suffering from an obstruction will stop eating and passing feces, and may move about with difficulty or not at all. Eventually, they will become listless and unresponsive, and may keep their eyes closed for long periods of time. Home remedies such as forcing the animal to swim in shallow water for a time and force-feeding mineral oil are rarely successful. A visit to the veterinarian is your best course of action if you suspect your gecko is impacted.

Calcium Deficiency

Calcium deficiencies can be a problem for fast-growing juvenile Leopard geckos. Deficiencies also occur with breeding females, who draw on their own body stores to produce eggs. The importance of adding calcium to a gecko's diet, and how to do it, are explained in chapter 6, "Feeding Your Leopard Gecko."

The signs of a severe calcium deficiency include shaking or tremors and a rubbery lower jaw. If you detect the condition in time, increasing the calcium in the Leopard gecko's diet can alleviate it. (It is difficult to detect the problem early on, but an animal who is not eating is a likely candidate.)

Liquid neocalglucon (available from most pharmacies) works very well to increase the calcium levels in your gecko's diet. A very small amount goes a long way: The average dosage is one drop per day for a couple of days, then one drop per week. This regimen often resolves the condition. The liquid is very sweet, and a gecko will readily lick the drop off the tip of his mouth. Consult a veterinarian to determine the proper dose for your individual gecko, which the vet calculates according to the gecko's body weight.

Severe cases of calcium deficiency could have permanent effects, such as twisted limbs and other body deformations. Prevention is the best solution. Be sure to provide your gecko with enough calcium in his diet.

Injuries from Fighting

If you decide to keep a group of geckos, rather than a single lizard or a male and female pair, they may fight. If you do decide to keep more than one gecko in a vivarium, make sure there is only one male. Males in the same enclosure *will* fight.

Some breeders sell juveniles whom they have identified as males and females, based on the temperature at which they were incubated (you will learn more about breeding for a specific sex in chapter 10, "Hatching and Raising Baby Geckos"). This way of determining sex can be reliable, but only if it is done properly. If you do buy juvenile geckos identified as males and females, be sure to keep a close watch anyway. They may not turn out as expected.

Leopard geckos do not do well in groups. If you keep a group of males together in the same enclosure, they will fight. In fact, even the females may have an occasional dispute.

If you are raising a pair or several juveniles together, you will need to keep checking them to watch for any fighting. If you suspect that you have more than one male, separate them immediately. If one gecko seems to hide more than the others, the others may be picking on him.

Even females can have disputes. When several geckos are kept in the same enclosure, the group will have a hierarchy, or pecking order. You can reduce the chance of problems by making sure you do not overcrowd your geckos and by providing the proper number of hiding boxes.

You should provide one hiding spot per gecko, with an extra one or two added for insurance. Be aware that the mere availability of a cave will not ensure that your gecko will use it; move or add hiding places until all of your pets seem satisfied with their homes. (See page 51 for a discussion of the amount of space a gecko needs.)

If there is a fight between males and the result is serious—bites or other obvious injuries—you will need to see a veterinarian as soon as possible.

Prolapsed Sexual Organs

Another hazard for males is prolapsed hemipenes. The hemipenes are the internal sexual organs of the male Leopard gecko. They are located behind the excretory opening, called the vent, at the base of the tail. Right behind the vent in adult males you will see two bulges. These bulges are the hemipenes.

Sometimes the males will evert the hemipenes (that is, turn the hemipenes outward or inside out), and on rare occasions one side may remain everted. The reasons a hemipenis might remain everted are unknown, but dehydration may play a part.

A hemipenis that remains everted needs attention right away. If the organ dries out, it will become necrotic (the tissue will die off) and must be amputated. While in transit to a veterinarian, keep the prolapsed hemipenis moist by spraying it with water and by placing the animal on a moist paper towel.

Although rare, a female gecko may have a prolapse of her reproductive tract. This also requires immediate veterinary care. Proper attention can correct this problem. Keep the area moist, as described above, on the way to the vet, so these internal tissues do not dry out.

Runny or Bloody Stool

Keep an eye on the stool of your gecko. It should appear dry and well formed. It is normal for the stool to have a small white part. If the stool appears runny or has blood in it, you will need to see a veterinarian right away.

Runny or bloody stools could be a sign of a bacterial infection or a parasitic infestation. You should take a fresh stool sample, along with the animal, to a veterinarian for analysis. Collect the sample with a plastic spoon and place it in a plastic storage bag for sanitary transport to your veterinarian's office.

To avoid disputes, provide one hiding spot per gecko, plus one extra.

Internal Parasites

Wild-caught geckos frequently have internal parasites that require a veterinarian's care to remove. There are many types of roundworms, hookworms, and protozoan and flagellate parasites that are common in the wild. A wild-caught gecko will require a fecal exam so a veterinarian can determine what type of parasites he may have and prescribe appropriate medications.

It is a good idea to have an annual fecal exam for your animal as a precaution, even if he is captive-bred. The exam, performed at a veterinarian's office, is usually inexpensive. It is well worth the trip. When getting a fecal exam, bring a fresh stool sample in a plastic bag. Collect the sample and bring it to the vet as soon as possible after it is voided. The vet will look for living parasites, so do not freeze the sample.

Treatment is often easy and successful. The proper treatment does, however, require a veterinarian's care.

Mouth Infection

Mouth infections can sometimes occur in Leopard geckos. An injury or an unsanitary habitat is frequently the cause of these infections. Fighting between males can lead to a mouth injury. When seizing prey, a gecko may injure himself on a rock or by accidentally grabbing bark when lunging for the insect.

Geckos can get mouth infections. Look for swelling around the mouth and take your pet to the veterinarian for treatment. (This gecko is showing off his healthy mouth.)

There is even a reported case of the spurs on a cricket's jumping legs causing a gecko's mouth infection. The veterinarian in this case recommended that the keeper remove the hind jumping legs of adult crickets before feeding them to his gecko. This practice may sound cruel, but the rear legs of adult crickets do pop off much the way an adult gecko's tail does. The crickets do not appear to suffer any discomfort (and, in fact, will happily begin eating immediately afterward if given the chance!). Pinching the fat portion of the cricket's hind leg with forceps will cause the leg to drop off the body.

The best way to spot a mouth infection is to look for swelling around the mouth area. You should be familiar with your gecko's general appearance. If there is a slight swelling, you will notice it early on and treatment can begin before the infection spreads.

Treatment usually includes cleaning the wound every day with a disinfectant, plus a course of oral antibiotics. To properly treat any infection, it is important that a veterinarian first culture the offending bacteria. The culture helps the veterinarian decide which antibiotic to prescribe for a successful treatment. If treatment begins before the veterinarian takes a culture, a misdiagnosis is possible. Different bacteria require different antibiotics. The wrong antibiotic will have no effect, and your gecko may not recover.

Respiratory Infection

Respiratory infections can occur if your Leopard gecko's environment is too cold for prolonged periods. Watch for labored breathing or mucus bubbles on the nostrils. Raising the vivarium temperature often corrects the problem. If it persists, visit the veterinarian.

Part III
Behavior and Breeding

Chapter 8

Your Leopard Gecko's Behavior

One of the best things about owning a gecko is observing her behavior. Geckos are interesting creatures and can provide you with hours of observational enjoyment. Your Leopard gecko is nothing like a human or even a dog or a cat. But that's okay. It's this uniqueness that makes it so special to have a gecko in your home.

Learn to appreciate your gecko's special ways by learning as much as you can about her and by taking every opportunity to observe her behavior. Soon you will come to realize that geckos are quite wondrous creatures who should be appreciated for the unique critters they are.

Hunting

Geckos are excellent hunters and are entertaining to watch as they capture and eat their prey. Pay attention to your gecko the next time you feed her. Geckos are opportunistic feeders and do not deliberately go searching for prey unless they are extremely hungry. But if an unsuspecting insect comes within their field of vision, watch out! Geckos rarely miss.

If your gecko is feeling hungry and she spies an insect, she will begin to stalk the insect much like a cat would stalk a mouse. She will move with a very deliberate and controlled motion, all the while focusing intently on her victim. Once she gets within striking distance, the gecko will take a second to get the insect directly "in her crosshairs," and then, in the blink of an eye, the insect will be inside the

They May Eat, but They Don't Chew

Unlike our teeth, lizard teeth are all the same size and shape. Most lizards, including geckos, have teeth that are cone-shaped. Geckos lose their teeth throughout their lifetime, but new teeth simply grow in to replace the old ones.

They use their teeth to hold on to an insect, which they then swallow whole, usually headfirst. Large insects are often crushed between the teeth several times; this ensures they are dead and may render them flatter and therefore easier to swallow. The process is not, however, "chewing" as we know it—reptiles swallow their food whole and do not break off small pieces in the process.

gecko's mouth. Sometimes, just before the gecko strikes, her tail begins to quiver intensely.

The next step in the process is to swallow the insect, which the gecko does with a few movements of her head. While lizards do not chew their food into smaller pieces before swallowing, particularly large prey might be crushed or even bashed against the ground after capture. Except for very small insects, most prey animals are swallowed head first. Many geckos will then lick their lips, almost as if to say, "Wow, that was good."

Geckos will stalk their prey like a cat.

Shedding

Another one of the gecko's interesting behaviors comes when it's time for her to shed her skin. Geckos molt several times a year, with younger, growing animals molting more frequently than adults. Just before molting, many geckos become

Geckos shed their skin several times a year.

less active. Then, as the skin begins to separate from the lizard's body, the gecko will try to help it along by pulling at it and swallowing it whole.

Geckos can often be seen trying to pull the most stubborn pieces of skin off their toes, much as a dog would try to chew a burr out of her fur. If you keep amphibians such as frogs and salamanders as pets, you will notice that most will consume their shed skins. Geckos and other lizards do not always do this, but in the wild, their discarded skins are eaten by beetles, millipedes, snails, and other invertebrates. You should remove any uneaten skin that you find in your gecko's vivarium.

Territoriality

Geckos, particularly males, are notorious for being territorial. In fact, male geckos will fight violently to protect their turf. The gecko prefaces an attack by threatening his foe with a bobbing of his head. This display is intended to bluff the rival into retreating without a fight, and is often successful.

The main motivation behind this territoriality lies in the gecko's mating instincts. By protecting his territory, a male gecko is also protecting his right to breed with any females who are in the area. In captivity, male geckos will fight whether or not a female is present—the instinct is still there.

Geckos are not particularly social animals, and they prefer to live alone.

Female geckos occasionally become territorial as well, driven by an instinct to have access to the best food supply.

Home Alone

Because we humans are such social creatures, it can be hard for us to understand animals who do not need the interaction of their own kind. In the wild, geckos are solitary creatures who establish their own territory where they live, hunt, and breed. Male geckos will fight vehemently to defend this territory from other male geckos, and, in fact, some will not tolerate the presence of other geckos at all except during breeding time.

You may feel a bit uncomfortable with the idea of keeping your gecko all by himself in a vivarium because you may have the notion that the gecko is lonely. If your gecko had the psyche of a human being—or even a dog or a cat—your notion would be correct. Most mammals thrive on the companionship of others, especially our domesticated friends.

Your gecko is a whole different critter, however. By providing him with a space that he can call his own, without other geckos to compete for food or space, you are actually doing him a favor! Geckos prefer to be alone most of the time. It is less stressful for them, and because stress can be damaging to a gecko's immune system, it is ultimately the healthiest way to keep them.

Some Geckos Are Clones

Oddly enough, some gecko species are *parthenogenic,* which means the females can reproduce without a male partner. In these situations, the resulting offspring are sometimes genetic clones of the female.

It is surmised that nature created this ability to help the species survive during times when the gecko population is low and mates are few and far between. Parthenogenic species, such as the widely transplanted Indo-Pacific gecko *(Hemidactylus garnotii),* are particularly efficient colonizers, requiring only a single female to establish a new colony. Parthenogenesis has also been observed in other lizards, such as the North American Whiptail lizards *(Cnemidophorus* species), and in at least one snake species, the Flowerpot snake *(Typhlina bramina).*

Aphids, and a surprisingly large number of other insect species, also dispense with males from time to time. Both they and certain fishes, such as the popularly kept Clownfish, can also change sex if the circumstances require.

Mating

Most novice gecko owners are not ready to take on the hobby of breeding their geckos, since this can be a time-consuming and complicated task. However, it is interesting to note some of the different behavioral patterns that relate to gecko courtship.

When male and female geckos are introduced, the male will usually vocalize to the female, making whatever sounds are inherent to his species. A circling ritual comes next, along with some head bobbing and tail writhing. This is the way male and female geckos get acquainted, and mating usually results soon after. Scientists also believe this courtship ritual might be instrumental in inducing ovulation in the female gecko.

Nesting

Female geckos are not devoted mothers the way female mammals are, but they are nurturing in their own way. When a female is close to egg-laying time, she will select a secure place to deposit her eggs. The arboreal species tend to glue their eggs high up in a tree so they hang vertically. Terrestrial species lay their eggs on the ground, usually in a specially constructed burrow or other secure spot.

Leopard geckos and the other members of their subfamily lay soft-shelled eggs, in contrast to the hard-shelled ones produced by other species. As with most gecko species, a typical clutch consists of just two eggs.

The females of some gecko species will actually protect their eggs, fighting with other geckos who get too close to the nest. In fact, both the male and female Tokay gecko will guard the eggs and show aggression to any other lizard who nears

> **Did You Know?**
>
> Some members of one gecko subfamily, *Diplodactylinae*, are *ovoviparous*, meaning that they give birth to living young.

the nest. Female Tokay geckos have been known to consume the eggs of other females, a fact that may help explain the evolution of this defensive behavior.

Hiding

Although hiding isn't exactly one of the most fascinating gecko behaviors to watch, it is nonetheless an important activity for the gecko. Hiding is an important behavior in geckos—so much so that animals who are not provided a hiding place may become ill from the stress and die. Nature has equipped geckos with the instinct to get out of sight when they are sleeping so predators won't make a meal out of them when they are most vulnerable.

Different species of geckos prefer to hide in different ways. Arboreal species, such as the Tokay gecko, tuck their bodies behind leaves and under peeling bark. Some terrestrial species, such as the Thick-tailed gecko, prefer to hide on the ground under leaf litter. Other terrestrial geckos, including the Leopard gecko, are happy to stash their bodies away beneath a piece of wood or a rock. Those with particularly well-camouflaged bodies, such as the Leaf-tailed gecko, merely flatten themselves against a tree trunk—in effect, hiding in plain sight.

A gecko who does not have a proper hiding place may become ill and die from the resulting stress.

Your Gecko's Personality

Geckos do not have the same kind of behavioral traits as mammals, but they do have distinctive personalities. Indeed, different species are inclined toward different temperaments. While Leopard geckos tend to be quiet and easygoing, Tokays are aggressive and hard to handle. Banded geckos prefer to hide all day under a rock or a piece of wood, while Day geckos want to be out in the sunshine, watching the world go by.

Gecko personalities are not only unique to their species, but also to each individual lizard. Anyone who has spent any quality time around geckos will agree with this.

Geckos are fascinating to watch, not only because they are beautiful, but also because they have real personalities. The best way to discover your particular gecko's distinct character is to quietly observe her. Keep her vivarium in a place that is relatively peaceful, yet where you spend enough time that you will notice her activities.

If you watch your pet closely, you'll discover all kinds of things about her. You will probably see that she has certain preferences when it comes to food. Your gecko may look nonchalantly at crickets and only hunt them when she's really hungry, but pounce on mealworms the instant you place them in her enclosure.

You will find that your gecko has preferences for certain foods and specific spots in her vivarium.

You may also notice that your gecko likes to perch in a certain spot in her vivarium, looking down over her enclosure like a queen observing her domain. Or she could be the type who prefers to lie around in her hiding place or under an overhanging leaf rather than take in the big picture.

If you have more than one gecko of the same species, you will clearly see differences in each individual. Every gecko is a unique being, with her own special preferences and characteristics. One of the most interesting and fun aspects of gecko ownership is discovering the subtle character traits of your individual pet.

The Outside World

You may think your gecko's world is limited only to what is going on inside her vivarium, but this is not true. I discovered this firsthand one day shortly after acquiring Gordon, my Leopard gecko. I had placed a white container of crickets on the floor near Gordon's vivarium, which is in my home office (a great place to keep your gecko's enclosure, by the way). As I sat at my computer working, I noticed that Gordon had come out of his hiding place and was standing with his nose up against the glass, staring intently in the direction of the cricket container. I glanced over at the container, wondering what he was looking at, and discovered that an army of tiny black ants had attacked my crickets! Thanks to Gordon's acute observation, I was able to rescue my crickets.

You may not have had the chance to experience anything quite like this, but if you pay close attention, you'll notice that your gecko is aware of the world outside her vivarium. If you ever have to move your pet's enclosure, you'll see plenty of evidence of her observational abilities.

When you move your gecko's enclosure from one place to another, you will probably notice a significant increase in her activity. If you have a nocturnal gecko who usually hides during the day, you'll see your pet come out of her hiding place and start exploring the edges of her vivarium with avid curiosity, looking out through the glass in an obvious attempt to figure out what's going on. It's also possible that your nocturnal gecko may become frightened by what is happening and will quickly sequester herself in her hiding place, refusing to come out until things have settled down.

If you have a diurnal gecko, she will also take note of the change in scenery. You'll see her looking around, noticing that her enclosure no longer has the same outside scenery as it did before. If she gets nervous, she may find herself a cozy leaf to hide under.

Even though the interior of her vivarium has stayed the same, this change in the outside world can be rather stressful for your pet. To help her adjust to her

There's no question that your gecko notices what goes on around her.

new surroundings, avoid handling her for several days before and after the move. You should also withhold food during that time because stress is particularly taxing for geckos with full stomachs. Let your gecko settle in before you offer her food in her new location.

Another example of your gecko's awareness of the outside world is how she reacts to other pets you may

> **T I P**
>
> Before you pick up your gecko's vivarium and move it elsewhere, remove the water dish and any other accessories that could injure your pet if they happen to topple over and fall on her during the jostling that always occurs with a move.

have. If you have a cat or dog and your furry pet likes to sit outside your gecko's enclosure and watch her, your gecko will surely notice. If the dog or cat sits quietly and is not threatening (and you have a particularly mellow gecko species, such as the Leopard gecko), this can be an acceptable arrangement. However, if your cat or dog runs around, jumps on top of the vivarium, or, worse, tries to break into it, your gecko will be stressed by what is going on outside her home. Keep your cat or dog away from your gecko's vivarium if the animal does anything other than sit quietly and observe.

As you can see, your gecko is very sensitive to changes in her environment. For this reason, it's best to always place the accessories and dishes inside the vivarium in the same place. Geckos are creatures of habit and expect to find their hiding places, water dishes, and other items in the same place every day. Redecorating just for the sake of change may be fun for you, but it will be very stressful for your gecko!

Change of Seasons

Just about every creature on the planet notices when the seasons start to change. The seasons are part of the cycle of life, and even tiny insects are sensitive to them.

Your gecko is no exception. Wild geckos respond to the changes in temperature and light that the seasons bring, so it's only natural that they should notice these things in captivity, too. In fact, people who breed geckos will create artificial winter and summer using controlled lighting to encourage their animals to breed.

Nocturnal geckos who have no source of artificial light in their vivarium are most likely to take notice when the sun begins to set noticeably earlier in the day during the fall, or later in the day during the spring. Even though the pets are indoors and have an artificial heat source, they also tend to be aware of the change in temperature from warm seasons to cool, and vice versa.

Geckos tend to be more active in the warmer months and less active as the weather turns cool.

You can tell that your pet is responding to the change in seasons by observing her activity. Geckos tend to be more active in the warmer seasons than the cooler ones, so you may notice a difference in your pet when summer's heat turns to autumn cool. She may begin to eat a little bit less and spend less time moving around her enclosure. Although wild geckos don't hibernate, they do have a reduction in activity during the cooler months. Make sure you compensate for this change in weather by providing an adequate heat source for your pet, and by feeding her less.

You may also notice a behavior change in your gecko when winter turns to spring. Your lazy lizard may start coming out from her hiding space more often and be a little more interested in those crickets and mealworms now that the sun is staying in the sky a bit longer. Enjoy your pet's subtle reactions to the seasons while still providing her with the heat she requires to stay healthy. Let her help you celebrate the changing seasons in her own, lizardlike fashion.

Handling a Leopard Gecko

Perhaps the most endearing quality of geckos is their behavior when they are handled. Unlike many other lizard species, geckos are very trusting. They may sit in your hand and be content, or they may slowly explore. They make slow, deliberate movements and are not prone to quick bursts of speed. Climbing up your arm and onto your shoulder is common. Be sure to sit very still so your gecko doesn't fall. You may want to wear a long-sleeve shirt, because a gecko walking up your arm will tickle and may cause your arm to be unsteady.

> **TIP**
>
> Take extra care not to handle your gecko's tail. The tail will easily snap off if a gecko is picked up or grabbed by the tail. Get in the habit of not touching your gecko's tail.

Always remember to wash well after you handle your gecko. I cannot overemphasize the importance of washing, particularly where children, the elderly, or immune-compromised individuals are concerned. While geckos are not generally dirty, they are animals. They may have walked through feces and have residue on their tails, or they may have defecated in a water dish and then walked through the dish. This can leave bacteria on their skin that can be transferred to you and make you ill. It is not necessary to fear this bacteria and avoid handling your gecko, but you do need to wash after handling her to be on the safe side. Commercial antibacterial soaps work very well for cleanup. Get in the habit of washing after handling your gecko or cleaning her enclosure.

Different geckos enjoy different amounts of handling. Always respect your pet's preferences about being picked up.

The amount of handling your pet will appreciate varies widely from individual to individual. It's important to remember that lizards are quite different from dogs and other mammal pets, and should primarily be appreciated through observation. Your gecko's reaction to being picked up will be easy to judge. Animals who want to be left alone will attempt to squirm out of your grasp or otherwise avoid you. Even a relatively calm gecko will eventually tire of being handled, so limit the length of your contact accordingly. Do not handle gravid females, or any gecko within a few hours or so after she has eaten. Very young animals are often quite shy and delicate, and breeding pairs may be upset if disturbed when their minds are set on procreation!

The best way to pick up your gecko is to gently cup your hand underneath her. Do not grasp your pet too tightly, and, after judging her reaction, allow her to explore your hand and arm. Keep a close eye on her if she climbs up your arm, so you can catch her if she falls, and watch for nervous behavior that signals her desire to return to her home.

Biting

Leopard geckos do not bite when they are handled carefully. While a bite is not likely, always handle Leopard geckos with gentle care and respect. You may not realize your movements are rough or too fast. Never grab a gecko's tail or grab her behind her head. Doing so will scare her and may cause her to bite.

In the unlikely event that a gecko's bite breaks your skin, be sure to clean the wound, apply an antiseptic, and consult a doctor if you are unsure about proper wound care. Pet owners should also have current tetanus vaccinations.

Chapter 9

Breeding Leopard Geckos

At one time, breeding any lizard in captivity was a rare achievement. Today, we know a lot about breeding Leopard geckos, and even first-time lizard breeders usually do quite well. Many people soon learn that having a healthy male and female in the same enclosure may be all you need to get fertile eggs. There are, however, things you can do to increase the likelihood of success.

It's also important to remember that any animal you breed is your responsibility, and this should not be taken lightly. Make sure you have plans to house all the babies, or have homes lined up for them, *before* you start incubating your first clutch of eggs.

Do your homework, as well. This chapter and the next one will outline the basics, but there's much more to know about breeding Leopard geckos.

Sexing Leopard Geckos

The most important factor in breeding is the obvious: You need a male and a female. Telling the difference between the two can be tricky. From above, male and female Leopard geckos look alike.

Checking the Vent Area

The only way to reliably tell if a gecko is male or female is by looking directly at the vent area of a sexually mature gecko. The vent is at the tail base, on the belly side of the gecko.

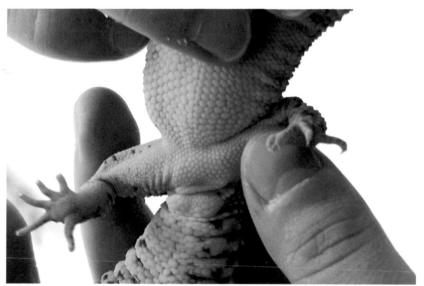

The lack of pre-anal pores and the bulges indicating hemipenes show that this gecko is female.

Where the tail base meets the body you will see a slit that the gecko uses for defecation and for copulation. (In common with all reptiles, except for the few parthenogenic species, Leopard geckos rely on internal fertilization for reproduction.) Directly above the vent, between the rear legs, is a series of pores that form a V shape. On female Leopard geckos these pores are very small and are not easily visible. Male Leopard geckos have large, easily visible pores that excrete a waxlike substance, possibly for use in marking their territories and in attracting females.

Below the vent, closer to the tail, males have a pair of bulges. These two bulges house the male gecko's hemipenis. When geckos mate, the male's hemipenis will be expressed externally; one side is used at a time. Comparing several geckos is the best way to see the difference, because the bulges are not huge. Once you see the difference, a quick glance will be enough for you to tell a male from a female.

It is easiest to determine sex in mature geckos. Once the gecko is fully grown, all of his or her external features are present, and the male's pores are visible immediately. It is possible to determine the sex of young geckos, but the conclusion is not reliable. A magnifying glass is helpful for determining sex in young geckos. You will likely need to examine many geckos this way before you can reliably distinguish the sexes.

Other external features sometimes differentiate a male from a female gecko. Males tend to be somewhat bulkier and have wider heads than females, but these differences can be subtle and are therefore unreliable.

If you purchase your gecko at a large expo or a herpetological society meeting, you may be able to have the breeder show you the difference between the sexes with animals they have on hand. Seeing the difference firsthand will make things much easier.

Proper Handling

Handling a gecko to determine the sex can be uncomfortable for the gecko, because you must hold the animal in a way he does not like. Turning a gecko upside down makes him feel vulnerable, and he will make every attempt to right himself.

By allowing your gecko to climb over your fingers, you may be able to guide him into a position where you can view the underside clearly. The trick is to spread your fingers slightly apart, below his vent area. You can gently restrain him with your free hand from above (or better yet, enlist some help), so that the vent area stays in view longer. Many geckos who fight against being turned upside-down will tolerate this quite well. Perform this handling with care.

Absence makes the heart grow fonder. Breeders find that separating and then reintroducing breeding pairs encourages them to mate.

Segregating the Sexes

Once you have determined the sex of your geckos, you must house the females separately from the males, and the males separately from one another. If not, the males will fight. The loser will hide, and the dominant male will pick on him every time he tries to emerge from his hiding area. The fighting could lead to severe injury or death of the smaller gecko.

Female Leopard geckos will generally get along without injuring one another, provided enough hiding areas are available and the enclosure is large enough. One male can be kept with one or more females. Some breeders keep one male with up to ten females. The best results, however, are often with one male and two females.

As a testament to the wisdom of the saying, "Absence makes the heart grow fonder," some breeders find that separating and then reintroducing pairs of geckos (or most other reptiles, for that matter) who have been housed together stimulates reproductive behavior.

Often the gecko does not fully cooperate and your clear view of the underside may last only a second, which is often not enough time. The risk of the gecko falling or losing his tail while you try to get a clear view of its vent area is a concern.

It is much easier to place the gecko in a clear container, such as a food storage container or a small plastic pet cage. Place the gecko in the empty container. Raise the container so that you can get a clear view of the underside. Take your time, look closely, and use a flashlight if necessary. This way, you can easily determine the gecko's sex.

Breeding Age

The next step is raising your geckos to the right age for breeding. Leopard geckos grow fairly fast and can be mature in about 1 year. Males will be ready sooner than females. Females need to grow large enough to be able to handle breeding.

It is best not to breed females before they are fully mature. While females can breed at an early age, they may not be able to handle the process of laying the eggs. The eggs are large for the gecko's size, and laying them can be a draining process for a young female, adversely affecting her growth and overall health. Most breeders wait until a female is between 18 and 24 months of age before allowing her to breed.

It is generally best to gauge a female's readiness based on size and weight, rather than age. Many breeders wait for a female to reach about 40 grams before considering her ready. Seasoned breeders will often wait until a female is even larger—50 to 60 grams. (One ounce is about 30 grams.)

A gecko's weight is very important as a way to assess readiness for breeding. If an underfed female is 18 months old but is still too small for the rigors of delivering a clutch of eggs, you should not breed her.

Small postal scales are useful for weighing geckos. Digital scales are more accurate and give a faster reading, but they are expensive. It is not necessary to have the gecko's exact weight for the purpose of breeding. The regular small, analog postal scales sold in office-supply stores will do. You will need a small container to weigh more active geckos. A paper cup works perfectly. Be sure to

In this picture, the smallest gecko is a newborn, the largest is an adult, and the one in the middle is 4 months old.

weigh the empty cup first and deduct that amount from the total when you add the gecko.

The scale will also come in handy when the eggs hatch. If you are raising young geckos together and some are not growing well, as based on their weight, separate them.

The Right Time of Year

The time of year is a major factor in the breeding process. A winter cool-down and hibernation period (also known as *brumation*) usually stimulates the breeding process. Autumn, when the days begin to shorten and temperatures drop, is the best time to begin a cool-down.

It is good to give the geckos some extra food before a cool-down period takes place, because they will not eat when they are hibernating. Make sure they have a good fat reserve. Their tails should look solid and thick. Offer some favorite foods and perhaps some extra treat foods, such as wax moth larva. This extra feeding will help ensure the geckos are in peak form before the rest period.

> **TIP**
>
> A month or so before hibernation is the perfect time to offer your gecko a special treat.

Hibernation Period

To prepare your geckos for hibernation, it is very important to let them clean out their digestive tracts. Food remaining in the digestive tract when the temperatures drop will not be digested and will eventually rot, causing the gecko to become ill and die.

In the wild, geckos stop eating when temperatures begin to drop and therefore have empty systems by the time the weather gets very cold. You must prepare your geckos in a similar way. Stop feeding your geckos ten days before the actual cool-down period. You should leave a water dish with fresh water, but do not offer food. Once the geckos have defecated, you can begin the cooling process.

Since you do not experience inside your home the major temperature changes that herald the seasons, you will have to create an artificial autumn. It is best to do the cool-down in stages, rather than expose your geckos to a very cold temperature all at once. A gradual change mimics what happens in nature and will enable them to acclimate and naturally slow down. The first phase of the cooling period can be a drop of about 10°F. Turning off the basking light and letting the vivarium reach room temperature is one way to begin this first phase.

After a few days at this temperature, the geckos are ready for the next step. The second phase is to reduce the temperature another 10°F to about 60°F (15.5°C) during the day. You can reduce the night temperature a few degrees more. After a few days, you can reduce the temperature another 10°F and leave the geckos at 50°F (10°C) for about five weeks.

These weeks are a period of rest for your geckos and for you. You can renovate the vivarium at this time, create a new habitat, or just take a break from your gecko responsibilities. The only thing you will need to do is check on them every few days to make sure they have fresh water available and that they look healthy. If they begin to look thin or are walking around a lot, you may need to bring them out of hibernation early.

Finding a place for safe hibernation temperatures can be a challenge. The idea of reducing the temperatures sounds simple, and the idea *is* simple. The hard part is the reality of being able to reduce temperatures in amounts that you can

You'll need to carefully control the temperature in the vivarium so your gecko can hibernate.

control in a heated home. Fortunately, with Leopard geckos there is some degree of flexibility in what temperatures will work to stimulate breeding activity.

For the first stage of cooling down, turn off the basking light or the heating elements. Although not absolutely necessary, you can also gradually change the photoperiod, aiming for approximately ten hours of daylight and fourteen hours of darkness. The second stage in a heated home could be moving your geckos to an unheated basement space. In most homes the basement stays cool, often in the 60°F (15.5°C) range, year-round. This temperature is perfect for the second stage of cooling.

The final stage, 50°F (10°C), can be tricky. Some homes have an unheated crawl space in the attic or closed-off, unheated sections. You may even consider asking a friend who may have a space available. Just make sure this space doesn't get too cold! If you are at all uncertain about this, purchase a *hi-lo type thermometer*, a simple device that marks the highest and lowest temperatures recorded over a specific time period.

Housing for geckos in this cool period can be very minimal. Plastic shoe boxes work well. One animal per box is best, but in a pinch a pair can share a box. Put paper towels on the bottom for substrate, and add a simple hide box and a water dish to complete the furnishings. The hide box can have damp peat or moss to raise the humidity.

> **TIP**
>
> If you do not intend to breed your geckos, there is no need for a hibernation period.

Even without extensive cooling, Leopard geckos may feel the triggers they need to successfully breed. Most breeders report more reliable success with cooling down their geckos, but breeding frequently occurs on its own, too.

Warm-up Period

When you remove the geckos from hibernation, a gradual warm-up is best. Raise the temperature 10 degrees at a time, leaving the geckos at each temperature step for a few days.

Once their hibernation enclosures are up to the regular warm temperatures you normally maintain, you may place the geckos back in their vivariums and begin feeding them. They should be eager to eat and will quickly be ready to mate. This is usually a good time to offer pinkie mice, especially to the females, who need enough energy for egg laying. (See the box on page 64 for some caveats about feeding pinkie mice.)

Also increase the amount of calcium you feed your females. They will be drawing heavily on their reserves to make eggshells. If there is not enough calcium in

After hibernation, your geckos will be active and hungry.

the females' diets, they will become calcium deficient and may metabolize the calcium in their bones.

It is generally safest to introduce the male into the female's tank, as he will be better behaved in a foreign environment. Males are usually territorial within their own vivariums, and while their aggression is usually directed toward other males, those in breeding mode may be unpredictable. However, if your female appears more aggressive or less nervous than the male, introduce her into his enclosure. If the pair has previously shared a vivarium, you can try placing them back in at the same time. Add the female first and leave her there for a few days, if the male seems particularly ornery.

The Mating

The mating may or may not take place when you are able to see it and confirm that it happened. Be sure to not interfere with or interrupt the geckos during this time. The male will approach the female and typically bite her on the back of her neck. This behavior is normal and she usually suffers no injuries. Once the male and female have lined up their vents, the male will evert one hemipene and copulate with the female.

As the eggs develop inside the female, you will notice her gaining weight. You can also see the eggs through the belly skin. The eggs will develop in pairs, although occasionally a gecko's first clutch is only one egg.

The female will lay her eggs in the hide box about one month after mating (but this time period varies widely). Watch closely and make sure you remove the eggs soon after the female lays them, because they can dry out quickly.

Setting up a Laying Box

To make sure you notice the eggs and can retrieve them quickly, you can set up a laying box. The laying box should have the entry hole on the side of the box rather than the top. This will enable the female gecko to expel some of the substrate—which should consist of a mixture of slightly moist (but not wet) sand, vermiculite, and sphagnum moss—while she is digging to lay her eggs. The substrate scattered outside the entry hole is a clear sign that the female has laid her eggs.

In the wild, egg laying generally begins in late winter or early spring. Warming temperatures and longer daylight hours trigger mating and egg-laying. The daylight hours may be the significant factor in the breeding habits of many captive geckos whose keepers do not provide a hibernation period—the sex organs of many reptile species attain breeding readiness in response to increasing day length.

The female will lay her eggs in a slightly moist, soft substrate.

More to Learn

Although the basics of Leopard gecko breeding are well known, the same cannot be said for the vast majority of reptiles and amphibians, including some of the Leopard gecko's rarer cousins. Therefore, the serious hobbyist should take careful notes on even the most mundane aspects of the reproductive process. In doing so, you may uncover principles that can be applied to the captive reproduction of other species. You may also discover subtle nuances that might enable you to improve upon current techniques.

While the effects of seasonal variations in photoperiod, temperature, and rainfall are fairly well researched, other factors that may affect the breeding process are not. In particular, changes in barometric pressure seem to affect the reproductive cycle of certain species, but details are lacking.

Another area calling out for research is the role of diet. It is well known that many animals experience wide variations in the availability of certain food items throughout the year. Many seem specifically to seek out particular foods at one time or another. Unraveling the effects of diet upon reproduction might provide the key to the husbandry of species that are currently challenging or impossible to breed in captivity.

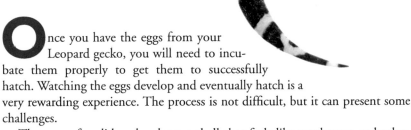

Chapter 10

Hatching and Raising Baby Geckos

Once you have the eggs from your
Leopard gecko, you will need to incubate them properly to get them to successfully
hatch. Watching the eggs develop and eventually hatch is a
very rewarding experience. The process is not difficult, but it can present some
challenges.

The eggs of eyelid geckos have a shell that feels like parchment or leather. The surface will give slightly to the touch. These eggs will also expand during incubation, as they absorb moisture through the shell. This expansion is a fantastic process to watch. The eggs expand a very noticeable amount and toward the end seem ready to burst. Since the eggs need moisture to expand and grow, you will need to provide the right amount of moisture in the incubation medium.

Choosing an Incubation Medium

The incubation medium is the material on which eggs are kept during the incubation period. There are several incubation mediums from which to choose. Vermiculite and perlite are the most popular.

Vermiculite

Vermiculite seems to be the most reliable and easiest substrate to use. Vermiculite is heat-treated mica. Mica is a mineral usually found in thin sheets that are very flaky.

When pieces of vermiculite are heated, they puff up and absorb large amounts of water. Since there are no organic compounds in mica, there is nothing to develop mold or fungus, making mica a very safe incubation medium.

There are different size grades available. One is larger and chunkier. This grade is generally used for gardening. Another grade is fine, like large-particle sand. Gecko and other reptile breeders usually use the finer grade, but the larger grade has been found to allow for more air circulation around the eggs. It is therefore the favored medium among professionals, especially for incubating eggs from species who inhabit arid environments, like Leopard geckos.

You can find vermiculite at any garden center or store that sells gardening supplies. A small bag goes a long way, since you need only a handful of vermiculite for an egg-incubating container. You can add about one part water to one part vermiculite, by weight. (See page 117 for more information on getting the right vermiculite-to-water ratio.)

Vermiculite makes a good substrate for incubating and hatching the eggs.

Perlite

Perlite is a naturally occurring rock (actually a form of glass) that is mined worldwide. It contains a good deal of water and, when heated rapidly, expands four to twenty times in size. The resulting expanded perlite is very porous and lightweight and chemically inert. Like vermiculite, perlite does not easily support fungal growth, allows for good air circulation, and is available in garden supply stores.

Choosing Egg Containers

Many things can be egg containers. Clear plastic food containers, the same kind in which stores package potato or macaroni salad, are best. You can buy these containers new or recycle those you have on hand from past trips to the grocery store.

Plastic food storage containers also work well, but it is best if they are clear. This way, you can see your eggs and keep an eye on them throughout their development without disturbing them. You can even watch for the hatching process without having to open the container and disrupt the hatchlings. Be sure the containers are clean before adding the incubation medium.

With good care and careful handling, you can find yourself raising a clutch of baby geckos.

Once you have chosen a container, put inside it about 2 to 3 inches of whichever medium you have chosen. Make a couple of depressions in the medium with your fingertip. The depressions should be deep enough that the eggs are about halfway buried into the mix. The top half of the eggs should remain exposed.

Moving the Eggs

Check the laying box frequently for the tell-tale signs of substrate scattered about outside the access hole. This will tell you the female has laid her eggs. If you see the substrate flying out or suspect the female is in the process of laying, it is important not to disturb her.

Once she completes the laying process, you may remove the box from the vivarium and carefully look for the eggs. Quickly harvesting the eggs will help ensure proper incubation.

If the female is still in the box, carefully remove her and place her back in her enclosure. You can softly push aside the peat moss and gently dig for the eggs. There should be two eggs, each about 1 inch long. It wouldn't be unusual for a first-time clutch to be just one egg. This first set or single egg might even be infertile—which would not be unusual or a sign of a problem.

Once the eggs are set into the incubating medium, do not move or rotate them.

If you aren't sure if an egg is fertile, incubate it anyway. Infertile eggs will begin to develop fungus within a week or so. However, viable eggs can also develop fungus, so follow the fungus treatment directions outlined on page 112 rather than discarding the egg right away. If the fungus returns rapidly and the egg becomes foul smelling, it is safe to assume the egg is not fertile and discard it.

Once you have uncovered the eggs, gently lift them from the laying box and transfer them to the incubation box. It is best to wear powder-free latex gloves when handling the eggs. Otherwise, oils from your skin might clog the egg pores and inhibit respiration. While many breeders do not take this precaution, it is an important safety measure.

In any event, be sure not to rotate the eggs when you pick them up. Unlike bird eggs, reptile eggs need to remain in the original laying position if the embryo is to develop properly. Place the eggs into the depressions in the incubation medium and softly close the top of the container.

The eggs are now ready to incubate. Using a marker, you can label the top of the container with the date the eggs were laid and from which pair of geckos, if you are breeding more than one pair. This tracking method will help you determine when the eggs will hatch and prevent you from pairing clutch mates together in the future. If you plan to sell the geckos you breed, buyers may want to know, for their breeding efforts, that they are buying different bloodlines and not related geckos.

Breeders sometimes will make a dot, in pencil, on the egg itself so that if someone moves the egg, they can place it back the way it was originally. Try not to handle the eggs.

Caring for the Eggs

For Leopard gecko eggs to hatch, they will need some specific care. The humidity of the air surrounding the eggs is the most important factor (see the box on page 113). In the wild, Leopard geckos lay their eggs deep underground. Even though the surface air may be dry, deep below the surface the soil is damp. If the air is too dry, water will pass out of the egg rather than into it. The egg will shrivel and the gecko growing within it will die. If you notice a small number of indentations, you will need to increase the humidity immediately. Minor indentations will not have an effect on the hatchling gecko if the conditions are quickly corrected.

Most Leopard gecko eggs will hatch in fifty to fifty-five days, but this period will be longer if temperatures are a bit cool and shorter at higher temperatures.

Fungus

If the air is too wet, the egg will develop fungus and the gecko inside will die. Sometimes a late-stage egg can begin to develop fungus for other, unknown, reasons. These eggs may still be viable.

If you notice a small amount of fungus beginning to grow on an egg, you may be able to save it. Gently wipe off the fungus and sprinkle an athlete's foot powder on the egg. These powders contain a fungicide and, when used in small amounts, work without harm to the gecko. Gently dab a small amount of the powder on the egg with a cotton swab. Watch the egg carefully over the remainder of the incubation period.

Avoiding Pest Infestations

Incubating Leopard gecko eggs can attract flying insect pests. Very small carrion flies often become serious pests. They will lay their eggs directly on the gecko eggs. The hatched larva will enter the egg via the air pores and kill the embryo inside.

Dead eggs attract carrion flies, but the flies may attack good eggs as well. Be sure to keep incubation containers clean and promptly remove dead eggs and hatched eggs with remaining yolk sacs.

Carrion flies resemble fruit flies but are slimmer and faster. They frequently infest cricket shipments, laying their eggs on the dead crickets. You may even find the small larvae on dead crickets, in the bedding, or on other material in the cricket containers.

Use fresh egg cartons or other cardboard to raise crickets, to avoid pest infestations in your gecko room.

Once established in a reptile room, carrion flies can be difficult to eliminate. Some breeders will keep flypaper in their rooms. Adding a bit of meat or gravy to the paper will increase its effectiveness. Commercially available flytraps are also very useful in this situation. Keeping cricket bins extremely clean will also help.

When opening cricket containers, the flies will often fly out of them. Opening the cricket boxes outside will let these flies leave the shipment box without entering your home. Use fresh egg cartons or

Maintaining Moisture Levels during Incubation

The moisture content of the incubation medium is critical in the hatching process. Ideal moisture levels vary widely from species to species and are determined by conditions in the animal's natural habitat. Too little water will cause the embryo to dry out and die, while too much can lead to fungal infections. Even minor variations in either direction can affect the development process and result in sickly or malformed hatchlings.

Leopard gecko owners are fortunate in that the eggs of this species are rather resilient and can tolerate minor mistakes on our part. It still makes sense, though, to pay careful attention to this stage of the incubation process. Maintaining the eggs at the proper moisture level will increase your overall hatching success and will provide you with a higher percentage of healthy, vigorous baby geckos.

Leopard gecko breeders have determined, after much trial and error, that the ideal moisture content for developing eggs is achieved by using a mixture of 1 or 1.5 parts substrate (ideally, coarse-grade vermiculite) to 1 part water, in a closed container.

Luckily, for those of us who are not mathematically gifted (many herpers, it seems!), there is a convenient way to measure the water and substrate. One milliliter of water weighs 1 gram. Therefore, if you are using a 1:1 formula, you only need to weigh your substrate and then add the same number of milliliters of water. For example, if your substrate weighs 20 grams, you add 20 milliliters of water to achieve a 1:1 ratio.

After mixing the water and substrate and adding the eggs to your incubation container, weigh the container (with eggs, lid, and substrate) and record that number. Thereafter, weigh the container weekly; any weight loss will be due to water evaporation. Simply add the amount of water lost back to the container to re-establish a 1:1 ratio. For example, if at week three you notice that the container weighs 1 gram less than it did during the previous week, add 1 milliliter of water (remember, 1 milliliter of water weighs 1 gram) to maintain your 1:1 ratio.

The lid of the egg container should not be perforated and should be kept closed during the incubation process. Opening the lid to visually check the eggs every other day or so will allow for enough air exchange. As hatching time nears, you will want to check the eggs daily, or even more frequently. At this stage the developing young will be using more oxygen, but their needs are easily satisfied by opening the lid for a minute or two every day. Assuming you check for hatchlings each day, the young will do fine in the closed container until you remove them.

other cardboard as a substrate in your own cricket containers, because the eggs of these flies may be on the egg cartons in the boxes in which crickets were shipped.

Maintaining Proper Temperatures

You must keep Leopard gecko eggs warm if they are to hatch. There are many ways to raise the temperature in the egg containers to the required level, which is about 80°F (27°C). If you have a warm spot in your home that is consistently at about 80°F, it will be warm enough for the eggs. If you have a room for your reptiles that is kept warm, you can place the egg container somewhere in the room, such as on a high shelf. The night temperatures can safely drop into the 70s (21°C or more).

At these temperatures, the hatchlings will almost certainly be all females (see "Incubating for a Specific Sex" on page 116 for more on this subject). For a more accurate and reliable method of temperature control, you can make or buy an incubator.

Incubators

Incubating eggs in an incubator makes the process more reliable. Home temperatures can fluctuate greatly and are often too low for successful incubation. An incubator will keep the temperatures even and at the proper levels.

Commercial Incubators

Manufacturers make incubators to suit every need. You can buy a Styrofoam incubator made for hatching projects for about $40. These incubators are well worth the money. There are several models available from a number of manufacturers. The standard model will hold several dozen eggs in plastic deli cups.

The next model above standard has a large window so you can check on your eggs without opening the unit and affecting the heat level. This is an especially important consideration as hatching time nears, because you will likely want to check your eggs frequently so that you can observe the hatching process. The top-of-the-line unit has a turbo fan built in to spread the heat evenly and reduce the likelihood of hot spots. Each unit has a thermostat. These thermostats can burn out over time, so be sure to check the temperatures daily using a thermometer.

Set up the incubator in advance. The red light will go on when the heat element is heating. Turn the adjustment knob until the light goes off, which means the thermostat is set for room temperature. Turn the knob up in very small increments. Watch the thermometer.

A standard Styrofoam incubator works well and is inexpensive.

Once you get to the desired temperature, leave it there. The adjustments take time, and any adjustment can take a while to level off, so set up the incubator and establish the right temperature before placing eggs inside it. Keep the incubator in a place where the room temperatures are stable.

There are other professional breeder-style incubators; the prices reflect the reliability and level of materials involved. High-price units can cool as well as heat. If you are incubating your eggs at 82°F (28°C) and it is 90°F (32°C) in the heat of summer, only these units can keep your eggs at 82°F. This temperature regulation is very important if you expect a specific sex.

Whichever incubation method you choose, a digital thermometer is a good investment. Accuracy in determining temperatures is paramount.

Homemade Incubators

If your budget is not very big but you do not trust your room temperatures, you can make an incubator for little money.

For many years, breeders have used old aquariums for incubating reptile eggs. An old aquarium and a standard aquarium heater will be sufficient to raise the temperature and keep it steady. You'll need to put a few inches of water in the aquarium so you can submerge the heater. The heater warms the water, and the water raises the air temperature to the level you need.

The sex of the babies is heavily determined by incubation temperature.

Place a brick or two in the water to have a surface on which to set the plastic containers (they should not sit in the water). Cover the tank with plastic wrap and you are set. You can also add some insulating material to the sides and top to make your homemade incubator more energy efficient.

You can even use the same general idea with a picnic cooler. Instead of filling the cooler with water, place a large jar full of water inside the cooler and put the aquarium heater inside the jar. This method works the same way as described earlier and should be better at holding the temperature than an aquarium. If you want to get fancy, you can cut a hole in the lid and tape in place a piece of Plexiglas or glass for a window. Being able to see your eggs without opening the incubator is very handy.

The mother of all homemade incubators is made from an old refrigerator. If you plan on having huge numbers of eggs, an old refrigerator is an excellent choice. It has shelving, is heavily insulated, and has doors that seal.

You only need to add a thermostat and a heating element. You can set the thermostat to send power to a light bulb or a heating cable for the heat. Mounting a digital thermometer to the outside with the sensor inside is the finishing touch.

Incubating for a Specific Sex

The sex of Leopard geckos is determined during the first two weeks of the incubation period. Incubation temperature, rather than genetics, determines the sex of the developing embryos.

By regulating incubation temperatures, breeders can produce offspring of a specific sex. Since the sex of geckos is not easily determined until they are several months old, regulating

> **CAUTION**
>
> Temperatures below 75°F (24°C) and above 95°F (35°C) can be fatal to the developing geckos.

incubation temperatures enables breeders to sell sexed juveniles with a certain degree of accuracy.

A high degree of accuracy in breeding for sex requires extremely accurate temperature maintenance. While certain temperatures do produce females or males, there can be some geckos in the group who are not the planned sex.

Eggs incubated at warmer temperatures produce higher numbers of males. As the temperature reaches a certain level, the number of males increases. The higher the temperature, the faster the incubation, too, so that eggs incubated at the upper end of the temperature range may hatch out in forty-five days or so, as opposed to the usual fifty to fifty-five days. To produce nearly all males, the eggs need a constant incubation temperature of 89°F (31.6°C) to 90°F (32.2°C).

Incubation temperatures below 84°F (28.8°C) produce mainly females, while hatchlings of mixed sexes are the rule when temperatures range from 84°F (28.8°C) to 87°F (30.5°C). As the temperature decreases, the number of females will increase. To produce mostly female geckos, the eggs need a constant incubation temperature of 78°F (25.5°C) to 79°F (26.1°C).

Incubating for Pigmentation

Research has shown that incubation temperature, in addition to determining the sex of geckos, affects the geckos' skin pigmentation. Cooler incubation temperatures tend to produce darker geckos. Breeders have now taken to adjusting the incubation temperatures to accommodate their needs. They adjust temperatures to produce the desired sex for the first phase of the incubation period, then reset the temperature for the desired effect on the gecko's skin pigmentation.

Incubation temperature will also affect your geckos' pigmentation.

The Hatching

When a Leopard gecko egg is ready to hatch, you will see dimples, or small indentations, form on the shell.

Shortly thereafter, the egg will most likely shrink down and collapse. The egg will look like it has gone bad, but it is really starting the process of hatching.

Soon you will see short slits in the shell. The hatchling makes the slits using a small egg tooth on the front of her mouth. The baby gecko makes quick bursts of side-to-side movements with her head, slitting the eggshell with every move. The nose will emerge, and then the gecko may rest for a short period. During this time the gecko absorbs the final reserve of her yolk sac.

Once the baby geckos have walked free from the eggs and have absorbed the yolk sacs, you can safely remove them from the egg cups, although some breeders prefer to leave them in the incubation cup until they have completed their first shed. The first shed happens very soon after the gecko is free from the egg. The high humidity of the incubation cup helps make sure this shed happens easily.

The newborn gecko eats the shed skin, which likely as she pulls it has some nutritional value, from her body, limbs, and tail.

Sometimes a baby gecko emerges from the egg with the yolk sac still attached. There are many reasons for the yolk sac to remain attached. If two geckos hatch out at the same time, one may begin running about while the other is still in the shell. The movement of the first hatchling can stress the second hatchling and force her to flee the egg early.

The hatchling slits open the egg using a small egg tooth on the front of her mouth. She emerges snout first.

Geckos who leave the egg with a yolk sac attached should be handled gently or, preferably, not at all. They will need to be kept moist, so line the incubation chamber with damp paper towels. If unhatched eggs remain, you should very gently move the hatchling to another container; that way, new hatchlings do not injure the animal by causing her to run about with the attached yolk sac. Keep the affected hatchling in a quiet area, disturb her as little as possible, and the sac will usually be absorbed within a few days.

Disturbing the eggs while they are hatching can also stress the gecko and cause her to try to escape a perceived predator. Despite the loss of valuable nutrients, geckos who hatch early can still thrive. The best thing to do if the gecko hatches early is to leave the animal alone so she can calm down.

Stress on Hatchlings

Hatchling Leopard geckos are easily stressed. When alarmed, they will raise up on tiptoe while arching their backs. If really scared, they may emit a hissing screech. They will usually screech if you mist them with water. The screech strongly resembles a Hollywood monster movie sound effect.

Stress has a huge effect on growing geckos. It can slow growth and cause aggression between geckos. Reducing stress is easy. Avoid overcrowding your young geckos by keeping a maximum of two hatchlings in a plastic shoe box. Eggs come in clutches of two, so this number of geckos per box is manageable.

If you have more than one breeding pair, set up a few shoe boxes to raise your young geckos. Each shoe box should contain a paper towel for substrate, a shallow water dish, a shallow food dish, and a couple of humid hiding spots. Small pieces of cork bark or commercial caves work well. You can also use small plastic containers, as long as the hiding spot allows for a humid, dark area where each gecko can reside.

Keep just one or two hatchlings in a plastic shoe box as you raise them.

Raising Young Leopard Geckos

Once your hatchlings have absorbed their yolks and are moving about, you can transfer them to their new homes. You can keep your hatchlings in a plastic shoe box or in a small aquarium or commercial plastic, small-animal cage. Whatever the enclosure, you should maintain the temperature in the mid-80s F (about 30°C). You can individually heat each container with heating pads. Overhead basking lights also work, but if they are the only heat source, your geckos will never have a dark, nighttime period—which is a stressful situation for them. Unlike adults, hatchling geckos should not experience a nightly reduction in temperature. Use a thermometer to keep track of the temperatures and make adjustments accordingly.

If you keep the room at the proper temperatures, the hatchling boxes can be left without heating elements, but most homes are not in the mid-80s (about 30°C) all the time and require a separate heat source for a Leopard gecko. Temperatures in this range also work well for raising juveniles.

As young geckos grow, you can move them to larger enclosures. Be sure to watch the sex of geckos as they approach maturity. Separate all males and keep them alone. You can keep females in groups, as long as they have enough room and hiding areas.

The babies will need special care as they grow.

Learning More About Your Leopard Gecko

Some Good Books

Ackerman, Lowell, *The Biology, Husbandry and Health Care of Reptiles*, Vol. 2, BA Young, Inc., 1997.

Bartlett, Richard D., *Reptile Keepers Guides: Leopard Gecko and Fat-Tailed Geckos*, Barron's Educational Series, 1999.

Daniel, J. C., *The Book of Indian Reptiles*, Oxford University Press, 1992.

De Vosjoli, Phillippe, R. Tremper, and R. Klingenberg, *The Leopard Gecko Manual*, Advanced Vivarium Systems, 2005.

Mattison, Chris, *Lizards of the World*, Facts on File, 2004.

Pianka, Eric, and Laurie Vitt, *Lizards: Windows to the Evolution of Diversity*, University of California Press, 2003.

Warwick, Clifford, F. L. Frye, and J. B. Murphy, *Health and Welfare of Captive Reptiles*, Chapman Hall, 1999.

Zug, George R., Laurie Vitt, and Jonalee Caldwell, *Herpetology: An Introductory Biology of Amphibians and Reptiles*, 2nd ed., Academic Press, 2001.

Magazines

Reptiles Magazine
P.O. Box 6050
Mission Viejo, CA 92690
www.reptilesmagazine.org

Reptilia
Bisbe Urquinaona
34 08860 Castelldefels
Barcelona, Spain
www.reptilia.net

Herpetological Societies

Just about every state has one or more herpetological societies. Here, I've listed just the larger ones. It would be worth your while to investigate which groups might be meeting in your neighborhood. The Internet is a good place to search for local groups.

American Society of Ichthyologists and Herpetologists
Florida State Museum
University of Florida
Gainesville, FL 32611
www.asih.org

Chicago Herpetological Society
2430 North Cannon Drive
Chicago, IL 60614
www.chicagoherp.org

Global Gecko Association
c/o Leann Christenson
1155 Cameron Cove Circle
Leeds, AL 35094
www.gekkota.com

New England Herpetological Society
500 Columbian Street
Weymouth, MA 02190
www.neherp.com

New York Herpetological Society
P.O. Box 1245
New York, NY 10163-1245
www.nyhs.org

Society for the Study of Amphibians and Reptiles
P.O. Box 626
Hays, KS 67601-0626
www.ssarherps.org

Southern New England Herpetological Association
16 Roaring Brook Road
Chappaqua, NY 10514
www.kingsnake.com/sneha

Internet Resources

Association of Reptilian and Amphibian Veterinarians
www.arav.org/Directory.htm
This online ARAV membership directory lists members by state in the United States and by country or geographical region elsewhere in the world.

Fauna Topsites
www.faunatopsites.com
This is a giant clearinghouse for links to forums, articles, fact sheets, and breeders of reptiles, amphibians, and invertebrates.

Gecko File
www.geckofile.co.nr
Connect with other gecko lovers at this site. It offers a gecko forum, links to other gecko sites, a chat room, and a free e-mail hosting service.

Global Gecko Association
www.gekkota.com
The GGA is committed to promoting interest in the responsible captive care, wild study, conservation, and understanding of geckos. The site includes care sheets, photos, recordings of gecko sounds, classified ads, and links to reptile interest groups.

The Herp Vet Connection
www.herpvetconnection.com
This site has a list of veterinarians recommended by reptile and amphibian owners worldwide, as well as links to veterinary sites and organizations.

Kingsnake.com
www.kingsnake.com
This granddaddy of reptile and amphibian sites has links to care articles and suppliers, a photo gallery, message boards, classified ads, and news of herp shows and events.

Leopard Gecko
www.leopardgecko.co.uk
This British site for Leopard gecko newcomers and old-timers includes care articles, a hatchling guide, photo galleries, recommended books, a description of the various patterns and phases, and instructions for making your own vivarium.

Leopard Gecko Top Sites
usa.ultimatetopsites.com/general/LeopardGeckos/
This site lists pages and pages of breeders and suppliers. Follow the links and you will also find lots of photos, articles on care and breeding, and myriad exciting colors and phases.

Leopard Gecko.com
www.leopardgecko.com
The website of noted breeder Ron Tremper contains a wide variety of detailed care and breeding advice, beautiful photos, and an astonishing array of "designer" Leopard geckos offered for sale.

Melissa Kaplan's Herp Care Collection
www.anapsid.org
You'll find articles here about just about every aspect of herp care, including finding a veterinarian, conservation, emergencies, and zoonoses (diseases that can be passed from animals to humans).

Photo Credits
Isabelle Francais: 13, 15, 16, 28, 29, 71, 105, 110, 116
Bill Love: 1, 4–5, 8-9, 11, 20, 33, 34, 35, 38, 40, 41, 49, 51, 61, 63, 67, 69, 74, 80, 82–83, 85, 86, 100, 104, 108, 109, 112, 117, 118, 119, 120
Tammy Rao: 22, 23, 27, 31, 32, 36-37, 42, 44, 50, 52, 53, 55, 57, 60, 62, 65, 68, 73, 75, 78, 79, 84, 87, 90, 91, 92, 94, 95, 96, 97, 98, 102, 107, 115

Index

acclimation, wild-caught geckos, 47
activity levels, seasonal changes, 93–94
age
  breeding determinations, 99–101
  purchasing considerations, 41–42
  verification methods, 45
albino gecko, 29
albino patternless gecko, 30
amelanistic gecko, 29
amelanistic patternless gecko, 30
anatomy, 10, 14–18
Anoles, pet lizard popularity, 13
aquarium gravel, substrate material, 52
Armadillo lizard (*Cordylus cataphractus*), armorlike
  skin, 14
Ashy gecko, ship/luggage stowaways, 19
autonomous tail, gecko characteristic, 16

Banded gecko, 19, 21
barometric pressure, 106
basking light, vivariums, 53–54
behaviors
  biting, 95
  hiding, 89
  hunting, 84–85
  mating rituals, 88
  nesting, 89
  personality traits, 90–91
  seasonal changes, 93–94
  shedding, 85–86
  solitary animals, 87
  territoriality, 86–87
biting behavior, cautions/concerns, 95
bloody/runny stools, 79
bowls (food/water), cleaning, 61, 73
breeders, 28, 48–49
breeding, 96–106
brumation. *See* hibernation period

calcium, 18, 67–68, 77
captive-breed, versus wild-caught geckos, 46–49
carrion flies, egg infestation, 112, 114
caves, vivariums, 55–56
circle back gecko, 31

cleaning habitat, 56, 62
clones, parthenogenic females, 88
Cnemidophorus species (North American Whiptail
  lizards), 88
colors, variations, 28–35
commercial incubators, 114–115
conservation, 46–47
Cordylus cataphractus (Armadillo lizard), 14
crickets
  carrion fly risks, 112, 114
  feeding guidelines, 64–66, 80
  gut loading, 70
custom-built habitats, 60–61

Day gecko, 15, 18
diet, 18, 106
digestive tract obstruction, 76–77
Diplodactylinae family, 89
diurnal geckos, round pupils, 21

ears, 18
eggs
  care/maintenance, 111–117
  containers, 109–110
  desired pigmentation, 117
  endolymphatic sacs, 18
  fungus treatment, 112
  hatching process, 117–119
  hatching temperature, 111, 114
  incubation mediums, 107–109
  incubators, 114–117
  infertile indicators, 111
  laying box, 105
  locating/removing, 110–111
  low humidity recognition, 111
  moisture levels, 113
  pest infestation, 112, 114
  specific sex incubation, 116–117
endolymphatic sacs, calcium, 18
environmental issues, ownership, 46–47
Eublepharis angramainyu, Middle East, 21
Eublepharis fuscus, India, 21
Eublepharis macularius (Leopard gecko), 20–21
eyes, 17–18, 21

Fat-tailed gecko, *Eubleparinae* subfamily, 21
feeder insects, supplement coating, 71
feet, 15
females
    breeding age, 99–101
    fighting injuries, 77–78
    laying box, 105
    mating rituals, 88, 104–105
    nesting behavior, 89
    parthenogenic, 88
    prolapsed sexual organs, 79
    segregation reasons, 99
    sex determination, 96–99
    specific sex incubation, 116–117
    territorial behavior, 86–87
fighting injuries, 77–78
Flowerpot snake (*Typhlina bramina*), 88
food bowls, 61, 65–66
foods
    breeder's information, 45
    commercial insect types, 63–64
    crickets, 64–66, 70
    feeder insect coating, 71
    feeding guidelines, 64–67
    gut load crickets, 70
    pink mice, 64
    reproductive cycle influence, 106
    serving guidelines, 66
    supplements, 67–71
    water, 72–73
    wild-caught invertebrates, 71–72
fungus, hatching eggs, 112

Gekko gecko (Tokay gecko), 15–17, 19, 89
Gekkonidae, lizard family, 11
glass enclosures, vivarium uses, 50
grass (dead), substrate material, 52

habitats. *See also* housing; vivariums
    breeder's information, 45
    diverse types, 11
    environmental issues, 46–47
    Leopard gecko, 23–26
handling
    autonomous tail cautions, 16
    guidelines, 94–95
    Leopard gecko, 27
    sex determination concerns, 98–99
hatchlings, 111, 114, 119–120
head, 15
health
    assessment guidelines, 44–45
    pet observation importance, 75–76

health problems
    calcium deficiency, 77
    captive-bred versus wild-caught, 46–47
    digestive tract obstruction, 76–77
    fighting injuries, 77–78
    internal parasites, 80
    mouth infections, 80–81
    prolapsed sexual organs, 78–79
    respiratory infections, 81
    runny/bloody stools, 79
    Salmonella, 25, 58–59
    stress, 76, 119
heat mats, vivarium guidelines, 55
Hemidactylus garnotii (Indo-Pacific gecko), 88
hemipenes, prolapsed sexual organs, 78–79
herpetological society, 38–39, 75
herpetologists, wild-caught geckos, 48
hibernation period, 101–103
hide boxes, 56, 58, 61
hiding behavior, 89
high yellow gecko, 31
hi-lo thermometers, hibernation, 103
hobbyists, 28
homemade incubators, 115–116
hot rocks, avoiding, 54
"house geckos," stowaways, 19
household pets (other), safety issues, 62
housing. *See also* habitats; vivariums
    cleaning, 61–62
    custom-built, 60–61
    hibernation period, 103
    laying box, 105
    vivariums, 50–60
humans
    gecko associations, 18–19
    Salmonella concerns, 25, 58–59
humidity
    hatching eggs, 111–114
    vivariums, 56–57
hunting behavior, 84–85

incubation
    commercial incubators, 114–117
    hatching process, 117–119
    homemade incubators, 115–116
    mediums, 107–109
    moisture levels, 113
    pigmentation, 117
    specific sex, 116–117
incubators, 114–116
India, *Eublepharis fuscus*, 21
Indo-Pacific gecko (*Hemidactylus garnotii*)
    ship/luggage stowaways, 19
    parthenogenesis, 88

injuries (fighting), 77–78
insects
    commercially available, 63–64
    hunting behavior, 84–85
    natural diet element, 18
    supplement coating, 71
    wild-caught invertebrates, 71–72
internal parasites
    symptoms/treatment, 80
    wild-caught geckos, 47

Jacobson's organ, taste sense, 26
jungle gecko, 31–32
juveniles, fighting injuries, 77–78

lavender Leopard gecko, 32
laying box, guidelines, 105
Leaf-tailed gecko, hiding behavior, 89
leusistic gecko, 32–33
lid clamps, vivariums, 51
lifespan, Leopard gecko, 24, 25
lighting, vivariums, 52–54
liquid neocalglucon, calcium deficiency treatment,
    77
lizards
    Gekkonidae family, 11
    Jacobson's organ, 26
    ownership considerations, 12–13
    parthenogenesis, 88
    popularity growth reasons, 12–13

maintenance, habitat cleaning, 61–62
males
    breeding age, 99–101
    fighting injuries, 77–78
    mating rituals, 88, 104–105
    mouth infections, 80–81
    prolapsed sexual organs, 78–79
    segregation reasons, 99
    sex determination methods, 96–99
    specific sex incubation techniques, 116–117
    territorial behavior, 86–87
mating rituals, 88, 104–105
meadow plankton, wild-caught invertebrates, 71–72
Mediterranean gecko, stowaways, 19
melanistic gecko, 33
mice (pinkies), avoiding, 64
microhabitats, South African Rhotropus species,
    11. See also habitats
Middle East, Eublepharis angramainyu, 21
minerals, nutrition requirements, 67–68
Monitor lizard, vomeronasal organ, 26
morph. See phase
mouth infections, 80–81

Native Americans, human/gecko associations, 19
necrosis, skin condition, 56–57
nesting behavior, 89
North American Whiptail lizards (Cnemidophorus
    species), 88

observation
    gecko's awareness, 91–93
    health problem indicators, 75–76
orchid bark, substrate material, 52
outside world, awareness of, 91–93
ovoviviparous, Diplodactylinae family, 89
ownership
    age guidelines, 41–42
    captive-bred versus wild-caught geckos,
        46–49
    environmental issues, 46–47
    gecko purchasing sources, 38–40
    health assessment, 44–45
    Leopard gecko, 24–25
    questions for you, 12

paper towels
    replacing daily, 62
    substrate material, 52
parasites
    internal, 80
    wild-caught geckos, 47
parthenogenesis, female cloning ability, 88
patternless gecko, 33–34
patterns, variations, 28–35
perlite, incubation medium, 109
personality traits, 90–91
pests, egg infestation, 112, 114
pet stores, purchasing pros/cons, 39–40
phase, 28
plants
    vivariums, 57–59
    watering guidelines, 61–62
prolapsed sexual organs, 78–79

questions
    breeder's housing/feeding, 45
    lizard ownership, 12

removable roofs, tunnels/caves, 56
reptile expos, purchasing pros/cons, 40
reptiles, gecko similarities/differences, 14–18
resources, 121–124
respiratory infections, 81
reverse strip gecko, 34
rocks, substrate material, 52, 59–60
roofs, tunnels/cave cleaning, 56
runny/bloody stools, 79

safety, 62, 94–95
Salmonella, health concerns, 25, 58–59
sand, substrate material, 52
screen lids, material suggestions, 51
seasonal changes, 93–94, 101–104
selective breeding, "wild" release concerns, 28
senses, gecko/lizard similarities, 14
shedding behavior, 85–86, 118
skin
    gecko/lizard similarities, 14
    necrosis, 56–57
    shedding, 85–86
smell sense
    gecko/lizard similarities, 14
    vomeronasal organ, 26
snow gecko, 34
solitary animals, 87
South African *Rhotropus* species, microhabitats, 11
spectacle, fused eyelid, 21
sphagnum moss, substrate material, 52
stools
    bloody/runny, 79
    internal parasite indicators, 80
stress
    causes/treatment, 76
    hatchlings, 119
striped gecko, 34–35
substrates
    cleaning/replacing, 61–62
    plant addition, 57–58
    vivariums, 52
succulents, vivarium plants, 57–59
supplements, 67–71

tails
    autonomous, 16
    characteristic traits, 15–16
    handling guidelines, 94–95
    re-grown/missing, 42–43
tangerine gecko, 35
taste sense, 14, 26
teeth, food holding device, 85
temperatures
    basking light guidelines, 53–54
    desired pigmentation, 117
    egg hatching, 111, 114
    hatchlings, 120
    heat mats, 55
    hibernation period, 101–103
    respiratory infection risks, 81
    seasonal changes, 93–94
    specific sex incubation, 116–117
    thermometer placement, 55
    warm-up period, 103–104

territorial behavior, 86–87
thermometers
    hi-lo, 103
    incubators, 114–117
    vivarium placement, 55
thermostats, heat mats, 55
Thick-tailed gecko, hiding behavior, 89
timelines
    egg hatching, 111
    food servings, 66
    habitat cleaning, 61–62
Tokay gecko (*Gekko gecko*), 15–17, 19, 89
traps, wild-caught invertebrates, 72
tunnels, vivariums, 55–56
Typhlina bramina (Flowerpot snake), 88

vent area, sex determination, 96–98
vermiculite, incubation medium, 108
veterinarians, locating, 74–75
vision sense, 17–18
vitamins, nutrition requirements, 68–69
vivariums. *See also* habitats; housing
    all-glass enclosures, 50
    awareness of outside world, 91–93
    basking light, 53–54
    caves, 55–56
    cleaning, 61–62
    heat mats, 55
    hide boxes, 56
    hot rocks, 54
    humidity guidelines, 56–57
    lid clamps, 51
    lighting, 52–54
    plants, 57–59
    relocating guidelines, 92–93
    rock placement, 59–60
    screen lids, 51
    size guidelines, 51
    substrates, 52
    thermometer placement, 55
    tunnels, 55–56
    wood cabinetry, 50
vocalizations, 16–17
vomeronasal organ, smell sense, 26

warm-up period, breeding, 103–104
water bowls, 61, 72–73
wild-caught, versus captive-bred geckos, 46–49
wild-caught invertebrates, 71–72
wildlife rehabilitation centers, 75
wood cabinetry, vivarium uses, 50
wood chips, substrate material, 52

zoos, veterinarian referrals, 75